American Presidential Candidate Spouses

Laurel Elder • Brian Frederick
Barbara Burrell

American Presidential Candidate Spouses

The Public's Perspective

Laurel Elder
Political Science
Hartwick College
Oneonta, NY, USA

Brian Frederick
Political Science
Bridgewater State University
Bridgewater, MA, USA

Barbara Burrell
Political Science
Northern Illinois University
Dekalb, IL, USA

ISBN 978-3-319-73878-9 ISBN 978-3-319-73879-6 (eBook)
https://doi.org/10.1007/978-3-319-73879-6

Library of Congress Control Number: 2017964613

Cover Credit: Image Source / Getty Images

Printed on acid-free paper

This Palgrave Macmillan imprint is published by Springer Nature
The registered company is Springer International Publishing AG
The registered company address is: Gewerbestrasse 11, 6330 Cham, Switzerland

Preface

First ladies in the United States have been the subject of numerous historical, social, and biographical works. Political scientists, however, have only marginally contributed to this literature. But as the women's rights movement has challenged conventional conceptions of women's roles in the political life of the nation and as an ever increasing number of women are seeking political leadership positions, the idea of a first lady engaged only in traditional activities has become an anomaly in the political world. Her role in the political process has increasingly become the subject of discussion and debate. The women who would be first lady and those women who have actually attained this position have increasingly had professional careers of their own and have become actively engaged in the campaign process as advisers to their spouses and as surrogates on the campaign trail. But traditional conceptions of their involvement in a presidential administration have constrained their activism in the White House. The idea that this country may soon have a man as first spouse has also stimulated conversations about the constraints and old-fashioned ideas surrounding this position.

As the political landscape has changed quite dramatically over the past few decades, several developments convinced the authors of this book that the time was right to undertake a project, more systematically exploring public opinion about first spouses. Political science has steadily become a more diverse field, recognizing the need to more fully explore issues of gender in politics, including how the public views the spouses of presidential candidates. The changing dynamics in the field has led to important scholarship examining first ladies and presidential candidate spouses by esteemed political scientists including Barbara Burrell, Marianne Borelli, and Lauren Wright. While each of their books has investigated the topic in varying ways, they have all contributed to a significant advancement of knowledge in this area, elevating it to greater prominence in the field.

Additionally, several major political firsts in recent years have magnified the significance of examining these political actors' public roles. In 2009 Michelle Obama became the first African American to serve as first lady. During the 2012 election Ann Romney became the first Mormon spouse of a major party presidential candidate. In 2016 former President Bill Clinton became the first male spouse of a presidential candidate nominated by one of the two major parties when Hillary Clinton secured the nomination of the Democratic Party. These high-profile events sparked a flood of articles, books, and other news features in the popular press about what these developments mean for American politics and society. Consideration of presidential candidate spouses should no longer be an afterthought among serious political observers.

Given this newfound interest in the life partners of presidential candidates, the authors of this study believed the time was right to coauthor a book that applied a more systematic examination than members of the media or punditry could provide. All three authors of this book have spent large portions of their career studying various aspects of how gender influences the American political process. Another central focus of the authors' research agenda has been investigating the political attitudes and behavior of the American public. This combination of scholarly interests led the authors to decide that a comprehensive account of public opinion toward presidential candidate spouses was a necessary addition to the research in this field of study.

What distinguishes this book from much of the previous scholarship is that it focuses exclusively on the American public's perspectives toward presidential candidate spouses. As the book explains in subsequent chapters, the role of the presidential candidate spouse in the US political process is central to appreciating how modern presidential campaigns function. Equally as critical in a democratic political system is understanding how the people themselves feel about various political actors including individuals who aspire to be first ladies or first gentlemen. What are the expectations the American people have for presidential candidate spouses? How have they reacted to the women and the man who have served in this role? These are just a few of the questions that this book seeks to answer. It does so through the combination of a theoretical framework the authors refer to as the "New Traditionalism" and an extensive collection survey data asking the American public about their feelings regarding the spouses of presidential candidates. These theoretical and empirical contributions go beyond what other books on the topic have attempted.

The finished product is a reflection both on the individuals who seek to become the first lady or gentleman and on the American public and its expectations for gender equity, campaign strategy, public policy-making, and the expectations for married couples in contemporary society. After reading it, the audience should get a more complete sense of not just how people view individuals like Hillary Clinton, Barbara Bush, Michelle Obama, Ann Romney, Bill Clinton, and Melania Trump, but also the bigger picture of how the public reacts to the behavior and actions of presidential candidate spouses in a more generalized way. In addition, to summarizing and contextualizing the evidence that has been collected in the past, the book also provides insight into what the future holds for public perceptions of candidate spouses. What follows is the definitive account of how the US citizens perceive presidential candidate spouses in the modern era of American politics, stretching from 1988 to 2016 and beyond.

Oneonta, NY, USA — Laurel Elder

Acknowledgments

We thank multiple colleagues in political science for their support and helpful feedback on various aspects of this book, including Bethany Albertson, Jim Buthman, Susan Carroll, Stefanie Chambers, Melissa Deckman, Amy Forster Rothbart, Caleb Goltz, Steven Greene, Farida Jalalzai, Mary-Kate Lizotte, Lanethea Matthews-Schultz, Janet Martin, and Zoe Oxley as well as the anonymous reviewers of the work. We would also like to extend our gratitude to the editorial team at Palgrave MacMillan for their support through the process of turning this project into the final book manuscript.

Laurel Elder extends her gratitude to Hartwick College for supporting this project. She was the recipient of the 2017–2018 Winifred Wandersee Scholar in Residence Award, which provided both time and financial support for the completion of this book.

Brian Frederick thanks the Center for Democratic Governance and Leadership and the Bridgewater State University Department of Political Science for its financial support of this project. He would also like to thank his family and his colleagues in the Bridgewater State University Political Science Department for their support and encouragement while writing this book.

Barbara Burrell thanks Laurel and Brian for asking her to participate in this research project and writing effort. She appreciates this opportunity to continue her thinking about the political life of first ladies and continues to find them excellent scholars with whom to work.

Contents

List of Figures

List of Tables

CHAPTER 1

An Introduction to American Presidential Candidate Spouses

The dividing line between the private and public lives of national-level candidates in modern political life has virtually vanished. In an era of social media, 24-hour cable news coverage, and rapidly changing journalistic norms candidates are evaluated on more than policy records and traditional qualifications for public office. They also are assessed on various aspects of their personal life. Whether they like it or not, candidates for high office in the United States, especially those individuals who aspire to the presidency, must confront the reality that they are judged in part by the company they keep, including family and personal friends. The individual closest to them, drawing the most scrutiny, is often their spouse.

Presidential candidate spouses are thrust into the public spotlight not because they are personally seeking a public platform or political power, but on the basis of a very private act of who they married. Former First Lady Laura Bush underscores the personal origins of the position of first ladies and would-be first ladies by remarking that "We are elected by one man" (The White House, Office of First Lady 2014).

Despite the personal origins of would-be first ladies and first gentlemen, the position of presidential candidate spouse has become undeniably political and influential. While the spouses of candidates have long been active in their husbands' campaigns for the White House, going as far back as the nineteenth century, it is only from 1992 on that presidential candidate spouses have come to play an especially prominent and strategic role in presidential campaigns (Vigil 2014). It has now become the norm for presidential

L. Elder et al., *American Presidential Candidate Spouses*,
https://doi.org/10.1007/978-3-319-73879-6_1

candidate spouses to pursue highly visible, very active, and strategically crafted campaign schedules—giving speeches, raising money, and appealing to key voting blocs (Burrell 2001; MacManus and Quecan 2008; Wright 2016). The public pays close attention to the activities of candidate spouses, feeling that it is through their actions and statements that they can better understand the genuine character and essence of the presidential candidates. This visibility and attention sparks the interest of voters and puts the candidate's spouse under the microscope of the public's gaze.

During her speech at the 2016 Democratic Convention, former First Lady Michelle Obama acknowledged how conscious she was of this scrutiny, even among the youngest Americans, remarking that "With every word we utter, with every action we take, we know our kids are watching us. We as parents are their most important role models. And let me tell you, Barack and I take that same approach to our jobs as president and first lady because we know that our words and actions matter, not just to our girls, but the children across this country, kids who tell us I saw you on TV, I wrote a report on you for school" (*Washington Post* Transcript 2016).

The larger question that arises from Michelle's Obama's recognition of this public spotlight is not only how young people view her as a role model, but also how the entire population views her and other spouses of candidates running for president. Why does the public view some presidential candidate spouses more favorably than others? What factors systematically underlie public perceptions of these high-profile figures as they carry out a role precariously situated between the public and private spheres? This book seeks to answer these fundamental questions through a multifaceted exploration of public opinion on would-be first ladies and gentleman over the past three decades, including an in-depth focus on candidate spouses in three key presidential elections: 1992, 2012, and 2016.

The period after the 2016 election and Michelle Obama's eight years as first lady are particularly important times for assessing public opinion toward presidential candidate spouses. During the 2016 presidential election, Melania Trump and Bill Clinton proved to be major departures from typical candidate spouses, albeit in markedly different ways, much as Hillary Clinton was in 1992 by going beyond the more traditional surrogate role, making it clear she would have an active policy role in the White House. Assessing public opinion of candidate spouses from 1988 through 2016, as this book does, allows us to identify key areas of stability and change in Americans' attitudes toward candidate spouses as the public is confronted with presidential candidate spouses who not only offer different conceptions of the role, as was the case with Hillary Clinton in 1992, but also embody historic firsts—the first African American spouse in the case of Michelle Obama, the first Mormon spouse in the case of Ann Romney, and the first male spouse in the case of Bill Clinton.

Presidential Candidate Spouses as Political Actors and Potent Symbols

At first glance it might not be obvious why a book on public opinion toward presidential candidate spouses is necessary. One might question whether public perceptions toward individuals aspiring for a position with no formal constitutional recognition is a wise investment of scholarly time and resources. Indeed, if voters are officially electing candidates for president and not the individuals they are married to, why should anyone care how citizens feel about them? This sentiment is certainly understandable. Despite these concerns, there are several notable reasons why scholars and other observers of American politics should want to know more about how the public evaluates the spouses of those candidates seeking the country's highest elective office.

The first reason is that presidential candidate spouses are highly visible and effective political actors. Many candidate spouses throughout history have taken part in presidential campaigns, but since the modern era of candidate-centered rather than party-centered campaigns their role has become even more vital and prominent (Burrell 2001). It is now typical for the spouses of candidates to make hundreds of appearances during presidential campaigns, to headline fundraisers, and to receive intense media attention in both news outlets and entertainment-oriented venues (MacManus and Quecan 2008; Stokes 2005). Candidate spouses have become important and prominent surrogates for the presidential candidates on the campaign trail (Burrell 2001). Thus, the public has many opportunities to learn about and develop views on the candidate spouses.

In her 2016 book, *On Behalf of the President*, political scientist Lauren Wright offers compelling empirical evidence that candidate spouses are not only prominent campaign surrogates, but are actually the most valuable presidential campaign asset. Candidate spouses are effective surrogates for a variety of reasons. One is that candidate spouses have the ability to "go personal" in a way no other campaign surrogates can (Wright 2016). Candidate spouses are uniquely positioned to draw on intimate, familial, and day-to-day experiences to give the nation a sense of who the candidate is as a person, as a father or as a mother, as a husband or as a wife, and in many other aspects of their life outside of the public's view. Thus, candidate spouses can vouch for the candidate's suitability to be president in ways no other campaign surrogate can.

There are numerous examples in recent history of these personal testimonials, a few of which are highlighted here. Ann Romney was credited with humanizing her husband, Republican presidential nominee Mitt Romney, during the 2012 presidential campaign. Mitt Romney had extensive credentials and leadership experience, but many observers questioned whether he could relate to the everyday challenges of Americans, due to his enormous wealth and his family's political connections. In her 2012 Republican Convention speech, Ann Romney spoke about how she met Mitt Romney at a school dance, why she fell in love with him, and how they had a real marriage and faced real problems together including her battles with multiple sclerosis (MS) and breast cancer. She concluded her speech by saying that similar to Mitt Romney bringing her safely home from the school dance, he would take America to a better place. She used her intimate knowledge of Mitt Romney as a suitor and a husband to make him seem more likeable and relatable to the public (Vigil 2014).

Melania Trump struck a similar tone in her infrequent campaign appearances on behalf of her husband Donald Trump. On November 3, 2016, before a crowd in the swing state of Pennsylvania, Melania Trump stated, "I come here today to talk about my husband, Donald, and his deep love and respect for this country, and all of its people. I have come here to talk about this man I have known for 18 years. And I have come here today, to talk about our partnership, our family, and what I know for sure in my heart about this man, who will make America great again" (Zorthian 2016). During the campaign, Melania Trump also drew on her personal knowledge of her husband to counter allegations that Donald Trump had sexually harassed women.

The 2016 election demonstrated that the role of humanizing presidential candidates is not a task relegated to female spouses only. On the contrary, Bill Clinton played a similar role during his wife's presidential campaign. As Lauren Wright describes it, Bill Clinton attempted to do for his spouse, Hillary Clinton, "what first ladies have done for decades: reveal the human face of the candidate through charming anecdotes and personal information" (Wright 2016, 8). During his Democratic Convention speech, he shared an anecdote about when he and Hillary dropped off their daughter, Chelsea, at college for the first time. "There I was, in a trance, just staring out the window trying not to cry and there was Hillary on her hands and knees, desperately looking for one more drawer to put the liner paper in. Finally, Chelsea took charge and told us ever-so-gently that it was time for us to go. So, we closed a big chapter in the most important work of our lives. As you will see Thursday night, when Chelsea speaks, Hillary has done a pretty fine job of being a mother." In this speech, Bill Clinton shed light on the personal side of Hillary Clinton that no other supporter or member of her campaign could replicate.

Presidential candidate spouses are also important agents in the campaign because they are able to appeal to different and frequently broader audiences than their spouses. Presidential campaigns understand the value of candidate spouses and have deployed them strategically, crafting the timing and nature of appearances to maximize their impact (Burrell 2001; MacManus and Quecan 2008; Wright 2016). In 1992, for instance, Barbara Bush was more popular among elderly people, females, and better educated Americans than her husband, George H. W. Bush, which guided the way the campaign used her star power during the campaign (Mughan and Burden 1995, 145). In 2016, Hillary Clinton's campaign dispatched Bill Clinton to rural towns across America to appeal to white men, a group the campaign presumed he would be able to connect with more effectively than the candidate herself (Karni 2016). As MacManus and Quecan (2008) argue, the performance of presidential spouses on the campaign trail has the potential to influence the success or failure of their spouses' campaigns.

One of the most prominent examples of a presidential candidate's spouse being deployed to target a specific voting demographic was President George W. Bush's 2004 reelection campaign team's highly visible efforts to woo female voters. With an enormously popular profile, it was logical for the campaign staff to rely on Laura Bush to play an instrumental role in its strategy to close the gender gap. Burrell's (2005) review of the 2004 presidential election noted that "First Lady Laura Bush was central to the specific appeals the Bush campaign made to women. She appeared in 30-second ads strategically placed on women-oriented Web sites" (42). These "ads included Laura standing next to the President as he announced that he 'approved the ad'" (42). This strategy proved successful as George W. Bush's support among women increased by four percentage points in the 2004 election compared to 2000.

Presidential candidate spouses can also influence perceptions of their spouses among voters. Borrelli (2001) has argued that candidate spouses have the power to enhance the image of their partners on the campaign trail and throughout the election season. Lauren Wright provides (2016) compelling experimental evidence of that effect; she shows that through speeches candidate spouses can improve public perceptions of their spouses and their spouses' agendas. Burrell et al. (2011) also show that favorable views of candidate spouses during the 2004 and 2008 presidential campaigns led Americans to view the presidential candidate more favorably, and conversely, that a spouse who garners little favorable support from the public can weigh down presidential candidates in the eyes of prospective voters. A similar series of studies reveal that spouses of presidential candidates can have an independent influence on vote choice even when controlling for candidate feeling thermometer ratings, party identification, and ideology (e.g. Mughan and Burden 1995, 1998; Tien et al. 1999). In the hotly contested campaigns of the modern political era, anything that helps enhance support for candidates is a plus, and thus the roles of spouses are crucial. As a result, understanding why the public responds more favorably to some spouses than others is not only strategically important information for any modern presidential campaign, but essential for a complete understanding of the poll ratings of presidential candidates and ultimately the outcome of presidential campaigns.

A final reason that candidate spouses are important political actors worthy of more scholarly attention than they have received is because they are in many ways running for the position of first lady, a position holding the potential for considerable power and influence within the president's administration (O'Connor et al. 1996). The position of first spouse is not outlined in the constitution, nor is it a paid political position, but scholars agree it is an important one in terms of national influence (Watson 2003). First ladies are close advisers to the president, they possess an unparalleled platform to raise awareness about issues they deem important, and they act as powerful role models for the nation. Thus, understanding the individuals who are poised to assume this powerful position is crucial.

In addition to being important political actors, there is value in studying presidential spouses because they embody an intriguing paradox in contemporary American politics. For the most part, presidential candidate spouses remain highly popular figures in an increasingly polarized and negative political environment. Study after study has documented growing ideological and partisan polarization shaping virtually every aspect of American politics (Abramowitz 2011; Campbell 2016). Gary Jacobson (2003, 2006) has shown how each respective president's approval ratings have become progressively more polarized. Partisanship is increasingly used as a negative lens for evaluating policy issues and current political figures (Abramowitz and Webster 2016). This rise in polarization has coincided with declining levels of trust in political institutions at the national level (Hetherington 2005; Hetherington and Rudolph 2015). Yet, candidate spouses and first ladies have shown a distinctive ability to remain above the political and partisan fray.

In other words, presidential candidate spouses are anomalous figures in contemporary American politics in terms of their popularity and their relatively broad appeal. This book seeks to unravel the puzzle and understand why so many presidential candidate spouses have been relatively immune to broader negative partisan forces shaping aspects of modern politics. It is instructive to learn why candidate spouses have been able to avoid falling victim to these trends to the same degree that other political actors and institutions have over the past generation.

In addition, studying public opinion toward presidential candidate spouses reveals the American public's values, thoughts about family, and evolving ideas about gender roles in contemporary society. As one 2012 *Newsweek* article about presidential candidate spouses stated, "They fuel expectations and satisfy longing, and they often become the repository of voters' hopes and fears about society writ large" (Cottle 2012). Presidential candidate spouses are objects of fascination even among those who are not politically inclined as evidenced by profiles of spouses featured not only in news outlets but in general interest publications and venues. Americans view candidate spouses as important role models and project onto them their expectations for modern women. Their clothing and style choices are the subject of media attention, as seen in the case of Michelle Obama (Matthews et al. 2015). Often their speeches generate tremendous amounts of buzz among political pundits and media observers alike (Vigil 2014; Wright 2016).

The public seems particularly interested in understanding whether contemporary candidate spouses fit with the traditional ideals of first ladies our nation has long embraced. As political scientist Kelly Dittmar (2015) writes, "The nation not only elects a president to the White House, but also a 'first family' that has long been expected to fit a 'traditional' American ideal in image, structure and relational styles." In this way presidential candidate spouses are cultural touchstones, particularly when it comes to the appropriate role for women. Hillary Clinton's self-presentation during the 1992 election as a working woman who was interested in having input on political and policy matters touched off a national conversation about the appropriate role and influence of working women, a conversation that remains contentious and emotionally fraught in the twenty-first century much as it did a quarter century ago.

In a very meaningful way, public evaluations of candidate spouses are also a reflection of the public's expectations for the presidency. The institution of the presidency in the US political system is highly masculinized (Borrelli 2011). The traditional role of candidate spouses has been to underscore and frame the masculine traits of their husbands, which in turn reinforces the gendered nature of the presidency and presidential partnership (Dittmar 2015; Duerst-Lahti 2014; Mandziuk 2017; Vigil 2014). Thus, the study of public reactions to candidate spouses provides important insights into the gendered expectations of the presidency and more broadly the gendered nature of power in the United States.

Distinctive Contributions of This Book

A growing body of scholarship from an array of disciplines as well as interdisciplinary viewpoints explores first ladies and candidate spouses from perspectives other than public opinion (Watson 2003). A number of important studies critically assess media coverage of first ladies (Beasley 2005; Gardetto 1997; Mortensen 2015; Templin 1999) as well as presidential candidate spouses (Bystrom et al. 1999; Dittmar 2012), finding that coverage is highly gendered. Across media platforms and election years, coverage tends to be more positive, sympathetic, and benign when first ladies and candidate spouses operate within the traditional gendered space of these roles, and much more critical when first ladies and candidate spouses operate outside traditional expectations.

Similarly, an increasing number of studies have empirically analyzed and critically deconstructed the speeches and self-presentations of first ladies and candidate spouses (Duerst-Lahti 2014; Mandziuk 2017; Stokes 2005; Vigil 2014). In her analysis of the convention speeches presidential candidate spouses have given from 1992 through 2012, communications scholar Tammy Vigil (2014) finds that spouses' speeches stick to traditionally feminine topics and perspectives, which work to reinforce the traditional masculinity of the presidency and the femininity of the role of candidate spouse. Mandziuk (2017) explores the ways the spouses of all the leading candidates in the 2016 presidential nomination process in both parties navigated the highly gendered terrain of presidential spousal politics and finds strong evidence that expectations that candidate spouses act as "good wives" remain alive and well.

Taken together, these studies provide vital information about the context in which candidate spouses operate. The focus of this book, however, is quite different. This study seeks to understand public attitudes toward these uniquely positioned political figures. While not a complete void, a thorough vetting of the political science literature reveals a very limited amount of research has been undertaken on this topic. Most closely related to the research goals in this book are studies examining public evaluations of first ladies. Scholars have been particularly interested in understanding public responses to Hillary Clinton as first lady as well as Michelle Obama, as each challenged the traditional expectations for the role of first lady in different ways (Burden and Mughan 1999; Burrell 2001; Knuckey and Kim 2016; Prysby and Scavo 2001; Sulfaro 2007). More recently, pollsters have turned their attention to candidate spouses, reflecting the increasingly visible roles of spouses on the campaign trail, although to this day public opinion data about presidential candidate spouses over the campaigns are spotty at best.

Collectively, the explorations of public opinion toward first ladies and candidate spouses reveal several themes on which this study will build: that Americans have historically shown a preference for traditional first ladies and would-be first ladies; that Americans view first ladies and candidate spouses through the lens of partisanship; that demographics including race and gender are sometimes significant factors in shaping evaluations; and that while views of first ladies and would-be first ladies are correlated with those of their husbands, the public also views them as independent political actors.

This book makes several important contributions to the public opinion literature on candidate spouses. Most previous studies have focused on understanding public attitudes toward candidate spouses within the context of one election (see Burrell et al. 2011 for an exception). In contrast, this book covers public evaluations of presidential candidate spouses across three decades, which provides a fuller picture of attitudes as well as greater analytical leverage in understanding the factors behind these attitudes. By expanding the scope of this study to candidate spouses across eight presidential elections, we are able to identify baseline trends, evolutions in attitudes over time, and aberrations from the norms in public opinion, which studies of candidate spouses during only one presidential election are unable to offer. Moreover, by conducting a comparative analysis of different types of presidential candidate spouses, this book builds a more comprehensive understanding of this dimension of gender politics in the contemporary era.

By engaging three decades of data, this book is also able to systematically investigate and advance multiple theoretical frameworks. The first framework concerns the distinctive set of expectations the public now has for the presidential candidate spouses, which we refer to as "the new traditionalism." This new traditionalism involves candidate spouses playing a traditionally gendered role, for example, signaling to the public that they are not interested in influencing policy (beyond supporting non-controversial policies focused on gender appropriate areas such as women and children) or acting as an adviser to their spouse and abandoning their own career or ambitions to act as a full-time parent and supporter of their spouse's electoral ambitions. At the same time, candidate spouses are expected to serve as an active surrogate on behalf of the presidential candidates, using their political platform to reach out to key constituencies and personally validate their suitability to occupy the highest political office in the land. Presidential candidate spouses who adhere to the norms new traditionalism prescribes tend to achieve greater popularity, while those spouses who violate those norms tend see their popularity suffer.

Chapter 2 in this book draws on prior research as well as extensive public opinion data to explore the concept of new traditionalism from multiple angles, and to identify key areas of stability as well as key areas of flexibility and evolution in terms of what Americans expect from candidate spouses. This book employs a natural experiment of sorts by assessing public reaction to candidate spouses who embody traditional expectations against candidate spouses whose self-presentation and/or actions challenge traditional expectations.

This book also adds to the understanding of public opinion toward candidate spouses by introducing the concept of incumbency advantage. While the idea of incumbency advantage features prominently in analyses of congressional and presidential candidates (Jacobson and Carson 2015; Mayhew 2008), it has not been applied to candidate spouses, nor assessed in a systematic way. By looking at four different candidate spouses who went on to campaign once again as incumbents—Barbara Bush, Hillary Clinton, Laura Bush, and Michelle Obama—this study is able to better isolate the impact and the conditional effects of incumbency advantage on public evaluations of candidate spouses.

By examining public opinion toward multiple candidate spouses, this book is also able to systematically assess the degree to which candidate spouses provide descriptive and symbolic representation to historically marginalized groups. While previous studies have looked at the role of sex, and to a lesser extent race, in shaping evaluations of candidate spouses, this study goes beyond such empirical endeavors to advance a theoretical framework for understanding the ways in which the descriptive aspects of candidate spouses influence public opinion.

Until 2016, all presidential candidate spouses in the general election were women. Through their high-profile campaign roles, presidential spouses are one of, if not the most visible women in the male-dominated world of presidential politics. Candidate spouses often give voice to the concerns and perspectives of women, offering women voters a type of representation and sense of connection to the political process that male presidential candidates simply cannot (Borrelli 2011; Mansbridge 1999). This book explores systematically whether women offer particularly warm evaluations of would-be first ladies and under what conditions this emotional connection is more or less likely to occur.

Along similar lines, this book explores public responses to candidate spouses who embody "historic firsts" (Simien 2016). Michelle Obama became the nation's first African American presidential candidate spouse in 2008. Given the dramatic underrepresentation of black women in national-level politics, her visibility throughout the 2008 and 2012 campaigns may have offered African Americans and women a particularly meaningful connection to national-level elections (Bobo and Gilliam 1990; Mansbridge 1999; Simien 2016). In 2012, Ann Romney became the first Mormon presidential candidate spouse. In 2016, Bill Clinton became the first male presidential spouse. This study pays careful attention to the way women, men, African Americans, and Mormons respond to candidate spouses who descriptively represent them and how this potentially symbolic representation influences evaluations.

Another theoretical framework this book develops concerns partisanship. Not surprisingly given the highly visible role presidential candidate spouses have come to play, partisanship has often shaped the public's evaluations of them, albeit less so than evaluations of the candidates themselves. The role of partisanship, however, is inconsistent and seems less strong for presidential spouses who stay comfortably within traditional expectations for this role. By systematically examining the role of partisanship in shaping evaluations of candidate spouses over time, this study is better able to isolate the effects of partisan polarization as well as identify the factors that lead the public to respond in a more partisan way to some candidate spouses than others.

A final theoretical framework advanced in this book concerns the tension between dependence and independence. Perceptions of candidate spouses are influenced by evaluations of the presidential candidates to a significant degree (Elder and Frederick 2017). Despite this relationship, the public views presidential candidate spouses as distinct political entities, and presidential spouses tend to be viewed more favorably by the public than the candidates themselves. This book explores the roots of this independence, the distinctive ability of candidate spouses to rise above the partisan fray and maintain an identity separate from that of their spouses.

Finally, this book contributes to the literature on candidate spouses by providing the first scholarly analysis of public opinion toward candidate spouses in the 2016 election. It outlines how Bill Clinton and Melania Trump challenged conventional expectations and much of the academic scholarship about presidential candidate spouses, albeit each in distinctive ways. Thus, to summarize, this book builds on existing research by providing an authoritative study that encapsulates both the theoretical and empirical foundations of public perceptions of presidential candidate spouses.

Data and Methods

The primary objective in this study is to gauge citizen perceptions toward US presidential candidate spouses. The book seeks to understand why some spouses have been more favorably received than others, to explore how attitudes about these women and one man differ across key demographics, and to identify the key factors shaping the public's attitudes. To accomplish these objectives, the book relies on a wealth of survey data from a variety of sources.

First, the book draws on aggregate-level public opinion data about presidential candidate spouses from the Roper Center for Opinion Research archives. These data are used to assemble average favorable and unfavorable ratings of all the presidential candidate spouses from 1988 through 2016. These data are also used to identify baseline trends in attitudes toward candidate spouses as well as aberrations in those trends.

The over-time analysis, which begins in 1988, captures changes brought about by the new role of presidential candidate spouse offered by Hillary Clinton in 1992. Although some candidate wives acted as surrogates for their husbands prior to the 1990s,[1] many scholars view the 1992 election as a break with the past in terms of the importance and visibility of would-be first ladies (Burrell 2001; Mughan and Burden 1995). Indeed, 1992 is the first time polling organizations such as the American National Election Studies asked about candidate spouses, signaling the increased prominence of this role in national elections. The 1992 presidential election also marks the first time a presidential candidate spouse, Barbara Bush, gave a prime-time speech at the party convention (Vigil 2014), setting the stage for what has now become a standard expectation for candidate spouses.

The book also draws on aggregate public opinion data to assemble a picture of what Americans want in a candidate spouse in general, as well as how the public reacted to the specific candidate spouses that this study covers. By drawing on Roper Center polling data, the book offers a comprehensive list of questions pollsters have asked during the campaigns about each of the candidate spouses, identifying the dominant themes.

Additionally, this book employs public opinion data to conduct individual-level analyses to better understand the demographic and political factors that shape reactions to candidate spouses. A major source of data for the individual-level analyses is the American National Election Studies (ANES). The ANES is a comprehensive, highly reliable data set that allows this study to make valid comparisons across time and develop a rich understanding of public opinion in most elections. The ANES has most commonly used feeling thermometer questions asking how warmly respondents feel toward candidate spouses, ranging from 0 (cold) to 100 (hot).

Unfortunately, the ANES has an inconsistent track record of including survey items about the spouses of the major party presidential nominees in the general election. The lack of inclusion of candidate spouses in certain years speaks to the way in which candidate spouses are not always viewed as important political actors. When the ANES has included measures of attitudes toward candidate spouses, as it does in 1992 and 2012, the book relies on it as the primary source for individual-level analyses as it provides the richest array of political, attitudinal, and demographic variables. For example, in 2012, ANES not only asked respondents to identify if they were Mormon, but their attitudes toward Mormons, which is helpful in understanding attitudes toward Ann Romney, the first Mormon presidential candidate spouse.

However, in 2016, the ANES only asked respondents to rate Bill Clinton but excluded any questions about Melania Trump. In this case, therefore, we rely on data from the Roper Center Data Archive to conduct such analyses. More specifically, we utilize a CNN/ORC International Poll from October 2016 that asked respondents to assess the favorability of the candidates and their spouses. While this data set does not have all the independent variables ANES contains, it does include variables crucial to our analyses including sex, race, ethnicity, age, education, partisanship, and ideology.

Finally, this book draws on original polling data gathered from a KnowledgePanel (KP) OmniWeb survey conducted by Gfk Custom Research LLC (Gfk) September 15–17, 2017 that was commissioned specifically for this project to fill in some of the gaps in knowledge concerning political attitudes toward candidate spouses. Almost all pollsters' inquiries ask what role Americans would like first ladies or first spouses to play, rather than focusing specifically on the role of candidate spouses. The Gfk survey questions ask Americans what they expect specifically from presidential candidate spouses. In particular, how important is it to Americans that the husbands or wives of presidential candidates campaign on behalf of their spouses? And do Americans think it is okay for candidate spouses to speak about their own accomplishments on the campaign trail, as opposed to the accomplishments of their spouse? The Gfk survey questions also explore whether spouses of presidential candidates should be viewed in the same way as other political figures who campaign on behalf of the presidential candidate or if they should be viewed with greater sympathy, given that candidate spouses have not explicitly chosen this path, but come to it through the decision of whom they married.

Overview of the Book

The next chapter, Chap. 2, develops the theoretical frameworks discussed previously and considers them in the context of public opinion data on candidate spouses over the past 30 years. Using over time data, showing approval ratings of presidential candidate spouses from 1988 to 2016 as well as a list of all the questions pollsters have asked of candidate spouses, Chap. 2 explores how Americans' preference for traditional candidate spouses has been challenged or reinforced by presidential candidate spouses, and, importantly, how the public has responded. Chapter 2 also considers how traditional expectations for candidate spouses have evolved and how modern spouses are expected to be quite active within the traditional frame. Chapter 2 also presents over time data to explore the conditional effect of incumbency bias and the growing polarization of American politics.

Chapters 3, 4, and 5 draw on the theoretical frameworks developed in Chap. 2 to provide in-depth analyses of public evaluations of presidential candidate spouses in three elections: 1992, 2012, and 2016. These three elections were selected as cases because they feature a good mix of candidate spouses with unique ground-breaking characteristics as well as more traditional candidate spouses, providing the variation and analytical leverage needed to fully explore our theoretical frameworks. Given that it is not practical to examine every election cycle in detail, these three elections provide an ideal mix of electoral contexts including both open seat and incumbent races. The three elections that are focused on in-depth in this book—1992, 2012, and 2016—provide the opportunity to examine two sitting first ladies, two spouses of presidential challengers, and two spouses of open seat candidates, while having even distribution along partisan lines represented by a Republican incumbent in 1992 and a Democratic incumbent in 2012.

Including two in-depth cases featuring incumbent first ladies (the 1992 and 2012 presidential elections) is important, as there are both theoretical and empirical reasons to consider incumbent presidential candidate spouses as distinctive cases. With the benefit of media spotlight for almost four years, incumbent first ladies are much better known than would-be first ladies. Most Americans can offer an informed opinion of them, which is not the case for would-be first ladies. Additionally, with the notable exception of Hillary Clinton in 1996, incumbent spouses tend to be very well liked. Incumbent spouses have had four years to craft and hone their public images, and they benefit from this experience with higher-than-average approval ratings.

Chapter 3 explores the presidential campaign of 1992, which broke new ground for spouses in presidential campaigns, with Hillary Clinton explicitly challenging the traditional norms of behavior that had been expected from American public when it came to would-be first ladies. She and her husband Arkansas Governor Bill Clinton embraced the theme of "two for the price of one," actively signaling to American voters that she would play a significant policy and political role in a Clinton White House. This deviation from public expectations cost Hillary Clinton in the eyes of the public, as her favorability ratings were among the lowest in the past generation. This chapter contrasts Hillary Clinton's polarized reaction from the public to Barbara Bush's enormous popularity. Barbara Bush embodied the traditional "good wife" model of first lady and was rewarded with an overwhelmingly positive reaction from public. Barbara Bush remains the most popular first lady over the entire time period covered in this study. This gap in favorability between spouses representing two very different visions of the modern first lady reinforced traditional gender norms of what conduct was acceptable in that role, which no doubt shaped the behavior of future presidential spouses. Despite her unpopularity relative to Barbara Bush, Hillary Clinton's controversial image did not prevent Bill Clinton from defeating President George Bush in the 1992 election. Along similar lines, President Bush was viewed much more negatively than his spouse. These results confirm another major theme in the book that while the images of the presidential candidates themselves influence how the public views the spouses, the candidate spouses are viewed as distinctive political entities in their own right.

Chapter 4 explores public perceptions of the 2012 presidential candidate spouses, Michelle Obama and Ann Romney. Although these two women had different backgrounds and embodied different personal styles, they embraced similar roles during the 2012 presidential election. Both were highly visible and gifted campaign surrogates, drawing on their unique personal knowledge of their husbands to make the case that they would make the best possible president. Both emphasized traditionally gendered themes such as the importance of motherhood and family in their convention speeches. Both signaled that they were not interested in influencing administrative decision or shaping policy. And, as a result, the American public had quite favorable opinions of both Ann Romney and Michelle Obama. While the intensely partisan political terrain of the 2012 election did constrain the popularity of Michelle Obama and Ann Romney, both women remained less polarizing and more popular figures than their husbands. Since these two spouses represent historic firsts, with Michelle Obama the first African American presidential candidate spouse (in 2008) and Ann Romney the first Mormon presidential candidate spouse, the analysis pays particular attention to the role of gender, race, and religion in public evaluations of these two women and finds evidence that both women provided meaningful symbolic representation to historically marginalized groups.

Chapter 5 examines public opinion toward Melania Trump and Bill Clinton in the 2016 presidential election. The chapter documents the distinctive ways each candidate spouse shattered the new traditional expectations Americans have for presidential candidate spouses. On the Democratic side with Bill Clinton, not only was he the first male presidential spouse in the US history, he also happened to be a former US president with a very unique and controversial political record in his own right. The prospect of a man as a potential first spouse provoked great media attention, underscoring the degree to which expectations for this particular role remain highly gendered. For the Republicans, Melania Trump, a Slovenian immigrant with an extensive modeling career, which became a major flashpoint during the course of the Republican presidential nomination contest, cast a very different profile than her predecessors. The scandal over her plagiarized remarks at the Republican Convention, as well as her markedly low key role in the campaign, also signifies her role as distinctive. As a result, the 2016 candidate spouses were the least well liked of all candidate spouses over the past three decades. Melania Trump was the single most unpopular spouse on record.

The concluding chapter, Chap. 6, summarizes the comprehensive set of findings on US public opinion toward presidential candidate spouses in the context of the central theoretical frameworks advanced in the book: new traditionalism, the condition nature of incumbency advantage, symbolic representation, partisanship and polarization, and the interdependent nature of public attitudes toward candidate spouses and the candidates themselves. It explores the implications of these empirical and theoretical findings for public opinion toward the current first lady Melania Trump as well as for how presidential candidate spouses will be viewed by the American public in future elections. The concluding chapter looks beyond the results of the 2016 presidential election by taking into consideration broader social and political trends and what they may mean for how the public views presidential candidate spouses. The chapter also offers suggestions for future scholarly research on the spouses of presidential campaigns.

Note

1. Eleanor Roosevelt, for example, did not campaign on behalf of her husband. Yet, President Lyndon Johnson's wife was strategically sent to campaign in the south during the 1964 campaign since she had broader appeal in that region than her husband (Tien et al. 1999, 160 and 150).

Bibliography

Abramowitz, Alan I. 2011. *The Disappearing Center: Engaged Citizens, Polarization and American Democracy*. New Haven, CT: Yale University Press.

Abramowitz, Alan I., and Stephen Webster. 2016. The Rise of Negative Partisanship and the Nationalization of U.S. Elections in the 21st Century. *Electoral Studies* 41 (1): 12–22.

Beasley, Maurine H. 2005. *First Ladies and the Press: The Unfinished Partnership of the Media Age*. Evanston, IL: Northwestern University Press.

Bobo, Lawrence, and Franklin D. Gilliam Jr. 1990. Race, Sociopolitical Participation, and Black Empowerment. *American Political Science Review* 84 (2): 377–393.

Borrelli, MaryAnne. 2001. Competing Conceptions of the First Ladyship: Public Responses to Betty Ford's 60 Minutes Interview. *Presidential Studies Quarterly* 31: 397–414.

———. 2011. *The Politics of the President's Wife*. College Station, TX: Texas A&M University Press.

Burden, Barry C., and Anthony Mughan. 1999. Public Opinion and Hillary Rodham Clinton. *Public Opinion Quarterly* 63 (2): 237–250.

Burrell, Barbara C. 2001. *Public Opinion, the First Ladyship, and Hillary Rodham Clinton*. New York: Routledge.

———. 2005. Gender, Presidential Elections and Public Policy: Making Women's Voices Matter. *Journal of Women, Politics and Policy* 27 (1–2): 31–50.

Burrell, Barbara, Laurel Elder, and Brian Frederick. 2011. From Hillary to Michelle: Public Opinion and the Spouses of Presidential Candidates. *Presidential Studies Quarterly* 41 (1): 156–176.

Bystrom, Dianne G., Lori Melton McKinnon, and Carole Chaney. 1999. First Ladies and the Fourth Estate: Media Coverage of Hillary Clinton and Elizabeth Dole in the 1996 Presidential Campaign. In *The Electronic Election: Perspectives on the 1996 Campaign Communication*, ed. Lynda Lee Kaid and Dianne G. Bystrom, 81–96. Westport, CT: Prager.

Campbell, James E. 2016. *Polarized: Making Sense of a Divided America*. Princeton, NJ: Princeton University Press.

Cottle, Michelle. 2012. Battle of the First Ladies: Michelle Obama vs. Ann Romney. *Newsweek*, November 9. Accessed July 22, 2015. http://www.newsweek.com/battle-first-ladies-michelle-obama-vs-ann-romney-63859

Dittmar, Kelly. 2012. Turning the Tables: Behind Every Successful Woman. In *Women and Executive Office: Pathways and Performance*, ed. Melody Rose, 231–258. Lynne Rienner Publishers.

———. 2015. Gender Expectations and the Presidential Partnership. Center for American Women and Politics, Presidential Gender Watch. http://presidentialgenderwatch.org/gender-expectations-and-the-presidential-partnership/

Duerst-Lahti, Georgia. 2014. Presidential Elections: Gendered Space and the Case of 2012. In *Gender and Elections: Shaping the Future of American Politics*, ed. Susan J. Carroll and Richard L. Fox, 3rd ed., 16–48. Cambridge: Cambridge University Press.

Elder, Laurel, and Brian Frederick. 2017. Perceptions of Candidate Spouses in the 2012 Presidential Election: The Role of Gender, Race, Religion, and Partisanship. *Politics, Groups, and Identities*. https://doi.org/10.1080/21565503.2017.1338969

Gardetto, Darlaine. 1997. Hillary Rodham Clinton, Symbolic Gender Politics and the New York Times: January–November 1992. *Political Communication* 19 (2): 225–240.

Hetherington, Marc J. 2005. *Why Trust Matters: Declining Political Trust and the Demise of American Liberalism*. Princeton, NJ: Princeton University Press.

Hetherington, Marc J., and Thomas J. Rudolph. 2015. *Why Washington Won't Work: Polarization, Political Trust and the Governing Crisis*. Chicago: University of Chicago Press.

Jacobson, Gary C. 2003. Partisan Polarization in Presidential Support: The Electoral Connection. *Congress and the Presidency* 30 (1): 1–36.

———. 2006. *A Divider, Not a Uniter: George W. Bush and the American People*. New York: Longman.

Jacobson, Gary C., and Jamie L. Carson. 2015. *The Politics of Congressional Elections*. 9th ed. Lanham, MD: Rowman and Littlefield.

Karni, Annie. 2016. Can Bill Clinton Win Back the Bubba Vote? *Politico*, July 26.

Knuckey, Jonathan, and Myunghee Kim. 2016. Evaluations of Michelle Obama as First Lady: The Role Racial Resentment. *Presidential Studies Quarterly* 46 (2): 365–386.

MacManus, Susan A., and Andrew F. Quecan. 2008. Spouses as Campaign Surrogates: Strategic Appearances by Presidential and Vice Presidential Candidates' Wives in the 2004 Election. *PS, Political Science & Politics* 42 (2): 337–348.

Mandziuk, Roseann M. 2017. Whither the Good Wife? 2016 Presidential Candidate Spouses in the Gendered Spaces of Contemporary Politics. *Quarterly Journal of Speech* 103 (1–2): 136–159. https://doi.org/10.1080/00335630.2016.1233350.

Mansbridge, Jane. 1999. Should Blacks Represent Blacks and Women Represent Women? A Contingent 'Yes'. *The Journal of Politics* 61 (3): 628–657.

Matthews, Delisia, Cassandra Chaney, and Jane A. Opiri. 2015. The Michelle Obama Influence: An Exploration of the First Lady's Fashion, Style, and Impact on Women. *Fashion and Textiles* 2 (26): 1–12.

Mayhew, David R. 2008. Incumbency Advantage in U.S. Presidential Elections: The Historical Record. *Presidential Studies Quarterly* 123 (2): 201–228.

Mortensen, Tara. 2015. Visually Assessing the First Lady in a Digital Age: A Study of Michelle Obama as Portrayed by Journalists and the White House. *Journal of Women, Politics and Policy* 36: 43–67.

Mughan, Anthony, and Barry C. Burden. 1995. The Candidates' Wives. In *Democracy's Feast: Elections in America*, ed. Herbert F. Weisberg. Chatham, NJ: Chatham House.

———. 1998. Hillary Clinton and the President's Reelection. In *Reelection 1996: How Americans Voted*, ed. Herbert F. Weisberg and Janet M. Box-Steffensmeier. Chatham, NJ: Chatham House.

O'Connor, Karen, Bernadette Nye, and Laura Van Assendelft. 1996. Wives in the White House: The Political Influence of First Ladies. *Presidential Studies Quarterly* 36: 835–853.

Prysby, Charles, and Carmine Scavo. 2001. Who Hates Hillary? Public Opinion Toward the First Lady, 1992–1996. *Politics & Policy* 29 (3): 521–542.

Simien, Evelyn M. 2016. *Historic Firsts: How Symbolic Empowerment Changes U.S. Politics*. New York: Oxford University Press.

Stokes, Ashli Quesinberry. 2005. First Ladies in Waiting: The Fight for Rhetorical Legitimacy on the Campaign Trail. In *The 2004 Presidential Campaign: A Communication Perspective*, ed. Robert J. Denton. Lanham, MD: Rowman & Littlefield.

Sulfaro, Valerie. 2007. Affective Evaluations of First Ladies: A Comparison of Hillary Clinton and Laura Bush. *Presidential Studies Quarterly* 37: 486–514.

Templin, Charlotte. 1999. Hillary Clinton as Threat to Gender Norms: Cartoon Images of the First Lady. *Journal of Communication Inquiry* 23: 20–36.

Tien, Charles, Regan Checchio, and Arthur H. Miller. 1999. The Impact of First Wives on Presidential Campaigns and Elections. In *Women in Politics: Outsiders or Insiders?* ed. Lois Duke Whitaker, 149–168. Upper Saddle River, NJ: Prentice Hall.

Vigil, Tammy R. 2014. Feminine Views in the Feminine Style: Convention Speeches by Presidential Nominees' Spouses. *Southern Communication Journal* 79: 327–346.

Washington Post Transcript. 2016. Transcript: Read Michelle Obama's Full Speech from the 2016 DNC. *The Washington Post*, July 25.

Watson, Robert. 2003. Source Material Toward the Study of the First Lady: The State of Scholarship. *Presidential Studies Quarterly* (2): 423–441.

The White House, Office of the First Lady. 2014. A Conversation Between First Lady Michelle Obama and Mrs. Laura Bush Moderated by Cokie Roberts at "Investing in our Future": A Symposium for Spouses on Advancement for Women and Girls in Africa, August 6.

Wright, Lauren. 2016. *On Behalf of the President: Presidential Spouses and White House Communications Strategy Today*. Praeger.

Zorthian, Julia. 2016. Read Melania Trump's Campaign Speech Addressing Cyberbullying. *Time Magazine*, November 3.

CHAPTER 2

Understanding Public Opinion Toward Presidential Candidate Spouses

This chapter develops further the major theoretical frameworks that guide the analyses of public opinion toward presidential candidate spouses: new traditionalism, incumbency advantage, symbolic representation, partisanship, and independence. It engages these theoretical lenses as a way to make sense of public evaluations of candidate spouses, from Kitty Dukakis and Barbara Bush during the 1988 presidential election through the 2016 election, when Bill Clinton and Melania Trump assumed the role of candidate spouse.

This chapter begins by discussing Americans' historic preference for traditional presidential spouses and then draws on an extensive array of public opinion data to explore what being a traditional candidate spouse entails in the twenty-first century. The chapter advances the concept of "new traditionalism" as a means of understanding why Americans have liked some presidential candidate spouses more than others, why some but not all first ladies have benefitted from an incumbency advantage in approval ratings when their husbands were running for a second term, and why pollsters have asked many more questions about some candidate spouses than they did for others.

The chapter further considers who in particular feels meaningfully represented by presidential spouses, developing the theory of symbolic representation, the idea that even though candidate spouses are not on the ballot they can offer a meaningful connection to presidential politics for historically marginalized groups. Finally, the chapter draws on over three

L. Elder et al., *American Presidential Candidate Spouses*,
https://doi.org/10.1007/978-3-319-73879-6_2

decades of public opinion data to explore the ways partisanship has framed perceptions of candidate spouses as polarization has increasingly shaped American politics. The chapter also explores the degree to which candidate spouses have been able to carve out their own independent images in the eyes of the public, shaped by, but not determined by, perceptions of their husbands or wife. Three decades of public opinion data support the idea that candidate spouses who are able and willing to carefully navigate within the new traditional expectations of first spouses are better able to rise above partisan polarization and maintain an image independent from their spouses.

Public Expectations for Presidential Spouses: The New Traditionalism

An important, consistent finding from research exploring public perceptions toward first ladies and candidate spouses is that the public prefers a fairly traditional first lady and candidate spouse (Benze 1990; Borrelli 2001; Burrell 1999, 2000; Burrell et al. 2011; Stokes 2005). In their study from the 1990s, Tien, Checchio, and Miller identify some of the key desired traits of traditional presidential candidate spouses. They state, "In short, it is acceptable to be a full-time wife and mother, hostess of the White House, supporter of feel-good causes, and goodwill ambassador to the world who stays out of policy" (1999, 155). What is less acceptable is for a presidential spouse "to exert an inordinate amount of influence on national policy decisions," whether it be through direct policy involvement or through private influence over their husbands (1999, 155). Tien, Checchio, and Miller conclude that "the more the public believes that the spouse has spent (or will spend) time doing the types of things 'a first lady should do,' the more warmly they feel towards her" (1999, 157).

In other words, a traditional spouse is almost, by definition, a woman and a mother; a traditional spouse is also a woman who pursues caring for her children and family as a full-time job rather than pursuing her own career or working for pay. A traditional spouse also refrains from major policy involvement or political influence. Yet, even within this traditional role there are expectations that presidential spouses engage in certain types of highly visible activities—that they champion "feel-good" causes, and that they take lead roles in White House ceremonies, state dinners, and trips abroad.

Aggregate public opinion data further clarify what Americans want in a presidential spouse and by extension presidential candidate spouses who are in many ways auditioning for the role of first lady or first gentleman of the United States. From time to time, polling organizations have asked Americans what it is they want or expect in a presidential spouse in the abstract, rather than asking about a particular first lady or candidate spouse. A *USA Today/Gallup Poll* conducted in October 2004 asked the most thorough set of questions on this topic. The survey not only asked Americans to identify what they felt were appropriate or inappropriate roles for the first lady, but they also asked Americans to imagine that the president was a woman and then to identify the appropriate and inappropriate roles for the ***husband*** of the president. Thus, the results of this survey, which are summarized in Table 2.1, allow one to tease out the active versus traditional expectations the public holds for the president's spouse and how these expectations differ or do not differ for first ladies versus first gentlemen. It should be noted that the results from this survey are now more than a decade old; nonetheless, they are useful in offering a degree of contextual understanding into the American public's feelings on this topic.

Table 2.1 shows that there are some roles Americans view as clearly appropriate and clearly inappropriate for presidential spouses, regardless of gender. A clear majority of the public does not want presidential spouses to play an active role in the president's administration. As Table 2.1 shows, 77 or 78 percent of Americans believe it is inappropriate for a first lady or a first gentleman to hold an official, paid advisory role in the president's office. A majority of Americans also think that it is inappropriate for the president's spouse to hold an unofficial and unpaid position in the president's office. In other words, even in the twenty-first century, Americans retain a strong preference for candidate spouses that keep a clear distance between themselves and the decision-making taking place in the White House. To the extent that the concept of a traditional spouse implies a hands-off approach to White House decision-making and policy-making, that is what the public prefers. As shown later in this chapter, presidential candidate spouses who violate these expectations pay a price in terms of their favorable ratings.

While the public does not want the president's spouse to be a White House adviser, the public does expect the presidential spouse to play an active and visible role. Americans are nearly unanimous in thinking it is appropriate for the president's spouse to act as the official hostess or host

Table 2.1 Public opinion on the appropriate role of the president's spouse

	Is it appropriate or inappropriate for the first lady to do the following?	*What if the president were a woman, do you think it would be appropriate or inappropriate for the husband of the president to do each of the following?*
How about serve as official hostess/host at White House events?	93 percent appropriate 5 percent inappropriate	91 percent appropriate 7 percent inappropriate
How about champion a non-partisan cause such as mental health or literacy?	91 percent appropriate 7 percent inappropriate	88 percent appropriate 9 percent inappropriate
How about serve as a trusted confidante to the president?	78 percent appropriate 20 percent inappropriate	81 percent appropriate 17 percent inappropriate
How about hold an outside, unpaid position for a non-profit foundation?	77 percent appropriate 20 percent inappropriate	77 percent appropriate 19 percent inappropriate
How about hold an outside, paid job in the private sector?	50 percent appropriate 47 percent inappropriate	64 percent appropriate 33 percent inappropriate
How about hold an official but unpaid advisory role in the president's office?	43 percent appropriate 54 percent inappropriate	43 percent appropriate 55 percent inappropriate
How about hold an official, paid advisory role in the president's office?	21 appropriate 77 percent inappropriate	20 percent appropriate 78 percent inappropriate
How about hold some type of elected office?	32 percent appropriate 65 percent inappropriate	44 percent appropriate 54 percent inappropriate

Source: Gallup/USA Today Poll, September (2004)

(in the case of a male spouse) at White House events. Similarly, the vast majority of Americans think it is appropriate for a presidential spouse to champion a non-partisan cause such as mental health or literacy. While serving as host/hostess or championing feel-good causes can be thought of as traditional duties, as they are in the service of supporting the president and viewed as feminine tasks, they are also duties requiring the spouse to be active and visible.

The public is more divided, however, on the extent to which the president's spouse should be able to operate autonomously—to engage in activities in pursuit of their own goals rather than activities to support their spouses and the Office of the President. Most Americans think the president's spouse should not hold elective office. What is perhaps even more telling is that Americans are roughly split on whether first ladies should be able to pursue their own career, with 50 percent thinking this is appropriate and 47 percent thinking it is inappropriate for the first lady to hold a paid job in the private sector, although there is increased support for first spouses holding unpaid positions at non-profit organizations.

These results verify that Americans hold more traditional expectations for first ladies than they do for wives/women in society more generally. Although this preference has not always been in evidence, Americans are now quite comfortable with the idea of women working, even if they have husbands that can support them and even if they have children (Saad 2017). As early as 1969, for example, 55 percent of Americans approved of a married woman working in business or industry even if she had a husband capable of supporting her. By 1998, this support had increased to 81 percent and has continued to increase since then (Saad 2017). In contrast to women in society more broadly, Americans are split on whether they think the president's spouse should be working. Interestingly, views on whether first ladies can or should have independent careers have grown more traditional rather than less traditional over the past 30 years. In May 1987 when *Gordon Black/USA Today* pollsters asked Americans the following question: Is it acceptable for the first lady to pursue a business career while her husband is president?, then 62 percent responded yes and 28 percent responded no. It is possible that after seeing a "career woman" serve as first lady, in the case of Hillary Clinton, that many Americans decided they preferred a more traditional first lady.[1] In this way, women who have been first lady appear to have shaped contemporary expectations for the role.

Finally, while Americans' expectations for presidential spouses do not differ much based on the sex of the spouse (Table 2.1), there are two revealing exceptions. Americans are more comfortable with a male presidential spouse working for pay and running for elective office compared to a female presidential spouse. In other words, Americans are more comfortable with male presidential spouses taking on autonomous roles and activities, clearly underscoring the traditionally gendered expectations for this role. This finding also suggests that respondents may be employing different expectations when evaluating male candidate spouses, an issue explored in more detail in Chap. 5, which focuses on public opinion toward Bill Clinton as well as Melania Trump during the 2016 presidential election.

When asked outright about whether they would like a first lady to be more active or more traditional, the public tends to be split, reflecting the conditional nature of the activity. The public wants the first lady to be a highly visible role model for women, to be an active champion of feel-good causes, and to be a supporter of the president as he carries out his duties and runs for office (as discussed more below), but a majority of Americans do not like the idea of a spouse who offers advice or tries to influence major policy initiatives. This study applies the label "new traditionalism" to these expectations. The concept of new traditionalism builds off of the work of Lauren Wright (2016) who critiques scholarship on first ladies for defining traditional as politically inactive. Wright, for example, finds that Laura Bush actually gave more policy-oriented speeches and more speeches overall during her time in office than did Hillary Clinton, despite many classifying Laura Bush as traditional and Hillary Clinton as untraditional. This underscores the tension of new traditionalism; people want presidential spouses to play an increasingly public role and an increasingly active role, yet to do so within a traditionally gendered context. These conflicting expectations create a difficult balancing act for presidential spouses. As the survey data presented later in this chapter establish, it is a balance some spouses have excelled in achieving while others have struggled to master.

New Traditionalism and Candidate Spouses

The survey questions discussed above (Table 2.1) focus on the appropriate role for presidential spouses. The expectations of new traditionalism, however, also apply to presidential *candidate* spouses, those individuals who are poised to become first lady or first gentleman. The public wants candidate spouses to behave in a traditional manner consistent with the expectations of first ladies, but the public also expects candidate spouses to be visible and active on the campaign trail on behalf of their husbands or wife. As communications scholar Tammy Vigil notes in her work analyzing the convention speeches of the presidential candidate spouses, "[a]s political activity among women continues to increase, so does the public's expectation for potential first ladies to be part of their husbands' campaigns. The participation of a spouse in a campaign demonstrates that person's likely role in the

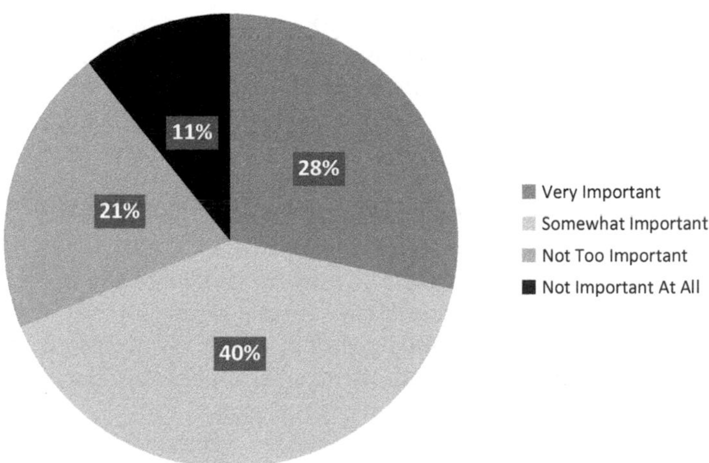

Fig. 2.1 Percentage of the American public believing it is important for husbands/wives to campaign on behalf of presidential candidates

White House" (2014, 330). Vigil goes on to argue that "Throughout a presidential campaign, the wife of a nominee is, in effect, auditioning for the role of first lady. As the role of presidential spouse has evolved, so have expectations by the electorate to hear from the helpmate to the would-be president" (2014, 331).

Original survey data collected specifically for this project through a KP OmniWeb survey conducted by Gfk Custom Research LLC (Gfk) September 15–17, 2017, lend further support to the view Tammy Vigil articulates.[2] As shown in Fig. 2.1, a strong majority of Americans, 68 percent, think it is important that the wives and husbands of presidential candidate spouses actively campaign on behalf of the candidate. This expectation is held by Democrats and Republicans alike. In other words, the expectation that candidate spouses be highly active is not being driven by Democrats while Republicans are satisfied with a more low-profile spouse. On the contrary, Americans across the partisan spectrum hold similarly high expectations for candidate spouses to be an active presence on the campaign trail.

The bipartisan expectation that candidate spouses be active on the campaign trail poses a particular dilemma for those who have careers and professional obligations, which is increasingly common for candidate spouses (Shoop 2010). Some candidate spouses have embraced traditional roles. For example, Barbara Bush and Ann Romney were both full-time wives and mothers. Other candidate spouses have given up their careers once they got married, as was the case with Laura Bush. Yet, an increasing number of presidential candidate spouses have come to the role with highly accomplished and ongoing careers. Hillary Clinton, for example, continued to work as a lawyer, while her husband was governor of Arkansas. Elizabeth Dole was president of the Red Cross, Cindy McCain was the chairperson of a successful family business, and Michelle Obama was a high-level administrator at the University of Chicago Medical Center (Shoop 2010). The question then, is how do candidate spouses balance the need to be a visible, active presence on the campaign trail with their careers? During presidential campaigns, they essentially need to relinquish their careers or at the very least put their career on hold and focus on supporting their spouse, or risk alienating the public.

This dilemma is exemplified by the case of Dr. Judith Steinberg Dean, the wife of former Vermont Governor Howard Dean. While Howard Dean did not ultimately become the 2004 Democratic presidential nominee, he was one of the top contenders. While he was running for the Democratic nomination and leading in the polls, Howard Dean's wife continued her medical practice in Vermont. Her absence on the campaign trail to continue her work was questioned in the news media and viewed negatively by some notable political observers. For example, Maureen Dowd, columnist for the *New York Times*, wrote an entire column speculating about whether her decision not to campaign actively for her husband would inflict damage on Governor Dean's bid for the nomination. Dowd (2004) contended that Judith Dean "is a ghost in his political career. She has never even been to Iowa, and most reporters who have covered Howard Dean's quest here the last two years would not recognize her if she walked in the door, which she is not likely to do, since she prefers examining patients to being cross-examined by voters and reporters." Dowd added further that "Even some who admired Dr. Steinberg's desire to stay focused on her own life, healing the sick, still thought it odd that she would be so thoroughly disengaged from her husband's" campaign. Dowd's sentiments toward Judith Steinberg Dean's low key role in her husband's campaign reflect a prevailing view among most members of the public, as revealed in the original survey data discussed previously, that the spouses of presidential candidates should be highly visible campaign surrogates during the election process. Had Howard Dean won the Democratic nomination in 2004, it is likely that Judith Dean would have faced enormous pressure to be much more heavily involved in his campaign.

The career accomplishments of presidential candidate spouses reveal another dilemma embedded in the expectations of new traditionalism, which is that while many come to the role with impressive educational and professional accomplishments, the American public is split on whether discussing their own accomplishments is appropriate. While the public responds favorably to candidate spouses discussing their roles as mothers or wives (Vigil 2014; Mandziuk 2017), the public is divided on whether it is appropriate for a candidate spouse to speak about his or her own accomplishments while on the campaign trail, with 53 percent believing this is appropriate and 46 percent believing this is not appropriate (Gfk Omni Survey 2017). The public's comparatively negative reaction to Teresa Heinz Kerry, who gave speeches highlighting her own achievements alongside her husband's achievements during the 2004 presidential campaign, further elucidates this point (Stokes 2005; Thurman 2004).

New Traditionalism and Favorability of Candidate Spouses

The concept of new traditionalism provides an important lens for understanding public evaluations of candidate spouses, and more specifically why the public likes some candidate spouses more than others. There is only one type of question asked consistently about candidates' spouses across the modern era, which is whether respondents have a favorable or unfavorable impression of the candidates' spouses. The 1988 presidential campaign is the first year this question was asked about both major party candidate spouses, Barbara Bush and Kitty Dukakis.

Figure 2.2 draws on polls archived with the Roper Center for Public Opinion research to display the average percent of respondents who identified each spouse as favorable or unfavorable across their respective campaign seasons. Since different polling organizations use different response options for their favorability questions, in that some explicitly invite respondents to say they are undecided while others do not, Fig. 2.3 depicts an adjusted favorability score. This measure recalculates the favorability score so that it only includes the percent of respondents who could actually give a positive or negative rating of the presidential candidate spouse.

Figures 2.2 and 2.3 reveal that with a couple of exceptions the spouses of presidential candidates are very well liked by the public. Such strong levels of support are unusual among presidents and other national figures in contemporary electoral politics.

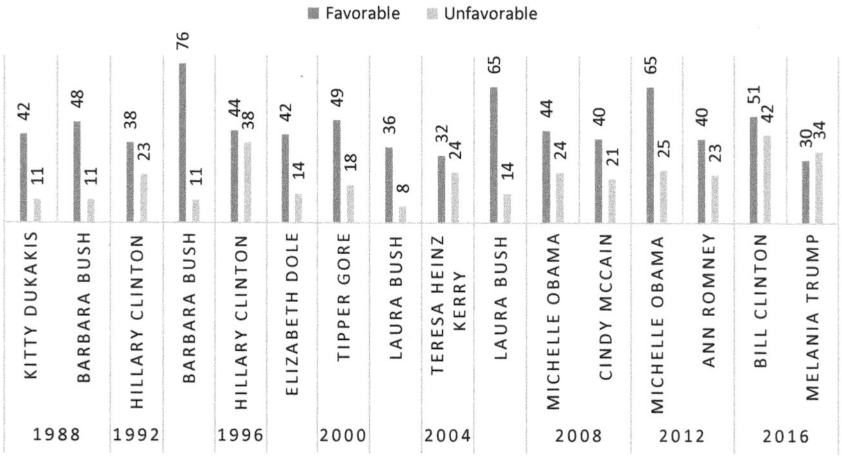

Fig. 2.2 Favorable and unfavorable averages of presidential candidate spouses, 1988–2016

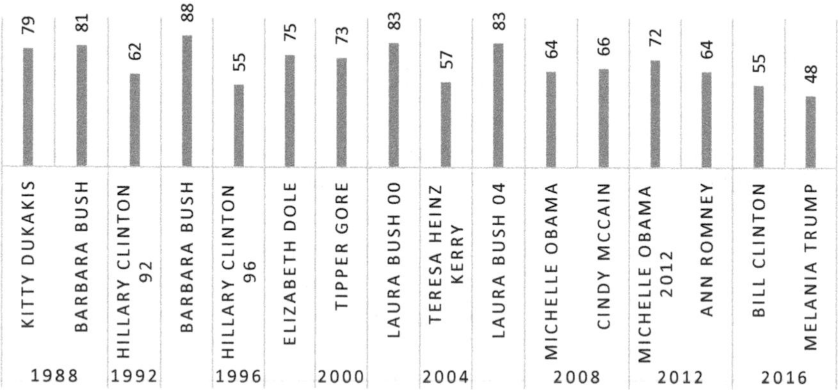

Fig. 2.3 Adjusted favorable averages of presidential candidate spouses, 1988–2016

These figures also reveal a clear bias toward new traditionalism. Of all the spouses in this study, the woman who achieved the highest favorable ratings was Barbara Bush. As Caroli (2010) has written, Barbara Bush was not only a traditional candidate spouse, but was more traditional than some of the first ladies who had come before her such as Betty Ford and Rosalynn Carter. She never pursued a career or paid work, but rather devoted her life to raising her children. At the same time, Barbara Bush pursued a very active role as a candidate spouse. She was an engaging presence on the campaign trail in 1988, and even more so in 1992 earning her the moniker "The Silver Fox." In 1992, she pioneered the now standard expectation that the first lady give a full address at the political parties' nominating conventions (Vigil 2014).

Not far behind Barbara Bush in terms of popularity is her daughter-in-law Laura Bush, the only other candidate spouse with adjusted favorable ratings in the 80 percent range (Fig. 2.3). Much like her mother-in-law, Laura Bush embodied new traditionalism as a candidate spouse and first lady, balancing a limited policy role with visible campaign advocacy. While she did speak out on policy issues in 2000 and 2004, most of her focus was on non-controversial topics like improving literacy and advocacy on behalf of women's and children's rights in Afghanistan (Caroli 2010; Dubriwny 2005), activities the public finds highly appropriate (Table 2.1). She served as an active presence on behalf of George W. Bush on the campaign trail, giving a public speech at both the 2000 and 2004 conventions (Vigil 2014).

In contrast to Barbara Bush and Laura Bush, Melania Trump stands out as the least popular spouse in the time series; she has the highest unfavorable average and the lowest favorable average (Fig. 2.2). She is the only candidate spouse in the modern era, with an adjusted favorable score of less than 50 percent (Fig. 2.3). The other candidate spouses with relative low adjusted favorable scores are Teresa Heinz Kerry, wife of 2004 Democratic nominee John Kerry, Bill Clinton in 2016, and Hillary Clinton in 1992 and even more so in 1996. A commonality about each of these less popular spouses is that they did not fulfill the expectations of new traditionalism in one or more important ways. Hillary Clinton and Bill Clinton indicated that they would be weighing in on policy matters and acting as advisers to the president, roles the public finds inappropriate (Table 2.1). In fact, during the 2016 campaign in response to questions about what role Bill Clinton would play in her administration, Hillary Clinton suggested he would be "in charge of revitalizing the economy" (Rhodan 2016). In the 2004 election, Teresa Heinz Kerry not only spoke about her own accomplishments, as discussed above, but she indicated that she would continue to pursue her own career as first lady, a choice half of Americans find inappropriate. And by staying away from the campaign trail for much of the 2016 election, Melania Trump failed to live up to the widely held expectation that spouses actively support their husbands on the campaign trail (Fig. 2.1). Each of these examples highlights how deviating from the expectations of new traditionalism places downward pressure on spousal favorability.

Candidate Spouses and Incumbency Advantage

Figures 2.2 and 2.3 also show that with the notable exception of Hillary Clinton in 1996, incumbent first ladies tend to be the most popular candidate spouses while non-incumbent spouses lag noticeably in their level of support from the public. Thus, a more complete and contextualized understanding of the role of incumbency in public evaluations of candidate spouses is crucial.

To better isolate the impact of incumbency on public opinion toward candidate spouses, this study calculates several additional statistics. First, it compares the approval ratings of incumbent first ladies to non-incumbent presidential spouses. Figure 2.4 shows that the average favorable ratings of sitting first ladies are 22 percent higher than the average for non-incumbent candidate spouses, 63 percent to 41 percent. When employing the adjusted favorable ratings to make this comparison, however, that advantage drops to seven percent. In other words, Fig. 2.4 indicates that most of the advantage sitting first ladies enjoy in terms of public support is simply a function of greater name recognition. However, even after accounting for the increase in name recognition sitting first ladies accumulate, incumbent first ladies remain seven percentage points more popular on average than non-incumbent candidate spouses.

This book advances the argument that the concept of incumbency advantage, typically applied to elected officials (Ansolabehere and Snyder 2004; Jacobson and Carson 2015; Mayhew 2008), also applies to public opinion

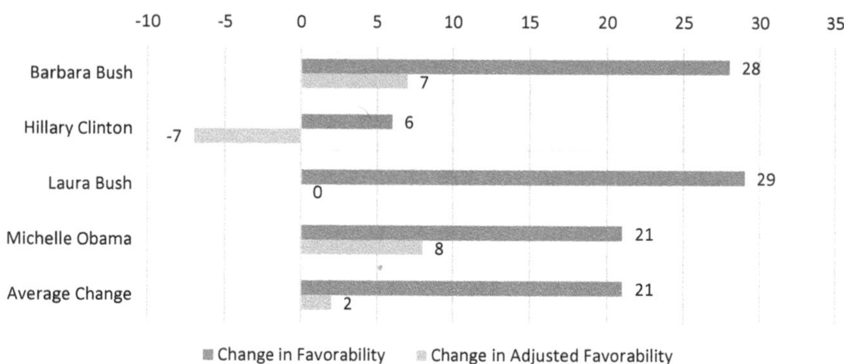

Fig. 2.4 Change in average favorability ratings for incumbent first ladies compared to first campaign

toward presidential spouses. Incumbent first ladies have the opportunity to utilize the stature, resources, and responsibilities of the Office of the First Lady to increase their visibility and strengthen their approval ratings among the public, much like incumbent members of Congress. The media coverage and institutional perquisites of office that come with holding the position of first lady give incumbent spouses an advantage in shaping their image and countering narratives about themselves that their non-incumbent counterparts do not enjoy. They also have the opportunity to demonstrate in a concrete way that they will comport with the public's expectations about how the first spouse should conduct herself/himself while actually serving in that position. In contrast, non-incumbent spouses are largely a blank slate from which the public must speculate over how they would conduct themselves once in office.

Looking at incumbency bias through specific cases, however, reveals that the effect of incumbency is conditional. Figure 2.4 also compares the favorable and adjusted favorable average of four incumbent spouses—Barbara Bush, Hillary Clinton, Laura Bush, and Michelle Obama—the first time they were campaigning on behalf of their husbands, with their second time in this role when they were campaigning as incumbent first ladies.

The results show that the benefits of incumbency are not automatic. Barbara Bush, already very popular when she campaigned for her husband in 1988, grew even more popular over the next four years, increasing her favorable average by 28 points and her adjusted favorable average by 7 points. A similar trend holds for Michelle Obama, who experienced an eight percent point increase in her adjusted favorable average, which is the largest increase among incumbent first ladies. Essentially, as people became more familiar with Michelle Obama, they developed a favorable impression of her.

Laura Bush also experienced a dramatic increase in favorable ratings from 2000 to 2004, but only in terms of absolute favorable ratings, not in terms of her adjusted favorable ratings. This divergence is largely because her adjusted favorability rating was already so high (Fig. 2.3). What made Laura Bush distinctive in 2000, the first time she campaigned as a candidate spouse, were her extremely low unfavorable ratings, which averaged only eight percent across the campaign season as well as the distinctively high percentage of people (56 percent) unable to rate her at all.[3] Her high adjusted favorability ratings in 2000, therefore, seem to reflect she was a benign non-entity during the campaign rather than a distinctively popular figure. By 2004, however, Laura Bush had clearly become a well-known and much admired woman.

This pattern was decidedly not the case for Hillary Clinton whose unfavorable ratings increased more than her favorable ratings from 1992 to 1996, which resulted in a decrease in her adjusted favorable ratings. The difference between Hillary Clinton and the other three incumbent first ladies is that Hillary Clinton embraced a policy role—taking on a leadership role in crafting health care policy while she was first lady—while the other three did not. It is possible that the toll on Hillary Clinton's image may have been less negative had her health care initiative been met with success rather than failure. On the other hand, the divisive nature of health care policy may well have damaged her approval ratings regardless, even if Congress had passed her proposed legislation, as illustrated by President Obama's experience in 2010 with the passage of the Affordable Care Act followed by a massive public backlash. What is clear is that by refraining from policy involvement and administrative decision-making and by championing issues well within the traditional sphere for women, Barbara Bush, Laura Bush, and Michelle Obama were able to avoid the backlash, which increasingly came to characterize public attitudes toward Hillary Clinton over her time as first lady, and receive the full benefits of incumbency. Thus, Fig. 2.3 shows that first ladies who adhere to traditional expectations receive an incumbency boost in approval ratings, while those incumbents who defy traditional expectations in some way fail to experience the same surge in popularity.

New Traditionalism and Pollster Inquiries

Another means of gaining insight into societal reactions to candidate spouses is to examine the number and type of questions pollsters asked about them during the campaign. Table 2.2 draws on polls archived at the Roper Center for Public Opinion Research to identify the number and nature of polling inquiries about presidential candidate spouses across their spouses' respective campaigns. In addition to showing the overall number of polls asked about each spouse, Table 2.2 also identifies the primary themes in tailored questions, by which is meant questions beyond the standard favorability questions asking something specific about one of the candidate spouses.

Table 2.2 shows that pollster interest in candidate spouses seems to have begun in earnest in 1992. In 1988, there was only one poll conducted across the entire campaign season that asked anything about candidate spouses, and in that case it was the basic favorability question. Starting in 1992, however, pollsters dedicated much more space on their

Table 2.2 Polls conducted about presidential candidate spouses during the campaign season, 1988–2016

	Number of poll questions asked	*Themes from tailored polling questions, e.g. questions asked specifically about a certain spouse*
1988 Kitty Dukakis	1	No tailored questions, only one basic favorability question
1988 Barbara Bush	1	No tailored questions, only one basic favorability question
1992 Hillary Clinton	60	Should she shape policy/be adviser? Her political ambition; Are Republican criticisms fair? Is she a good role model? How should she behave as first lady?
1992 Barbara Bush	22	Does Barbara Bush make one more/less likely to vote for husband?
1996 Hillary Clinton	113	Her influence in White House; Whitewater; White House Travel Office investigations; Media coverage; Her role as first lady
1996 Elizabeth Dole	39	Possible presidential run; Would she keep her job if first lady? Is she a good role model?
2000 Tipper Gore	18	Questions about depression disclosure, her work concerning music labels, homelessness, and mental health issues
2000 Laura Bush	10	Does she influence your vote for her husband?
2004 Teresa Heinz Kerry	18	Influence over her husband; impact of convention speech
2004 Laura Bush	17	Influence over her husband; impact of convention speech
2008 Michelle Obama	40	How much have you heard about Michelle Obama saying this is the first time in her adult life that she is really proud of her country? Does the opinion of Michelle Obama influence views of her husband?
2008 Cindy McCain	24	Does the opinion of Cindy McCain influence views of her husband?
2012 Michelle Obama	29	Did you watch her convention speech?
2012 Ann Romney	21	Did you watch her convention speech? Is it fair to criticize Ann Romney because she "hasn't worked a day in her life?"
2016 Bill Clinton	58	Bill Clinton's sexual transgressions; Bill Clinton's influence in his wife's campaign; Clinton Foundation
2016 Melania Trump	20	Impact on Trump presidency; Nude photos, whether she worked in the USA illegally, plagiarism of convention speech

Note: Head-to-head questions about which spouse would be preferred as first lady, president, or role model are not included. Roper Center for Public Opinion Research database was searched for each candidate spouse from January 1 through Election Day for each presidential election year surveys to querying the public about candidate spouses. Taken as a whole, Table 2.2 indicates that pollsters ask more questions when would-be presidential spouses are involved in scandals or defy expectations of traditional first ladies and fewer questions when spouses carry out traditional expectations for the role of candidate spouse, which, in and of itself, is revealing of Americans' expectation for traditionalism in candidate spouses.

At the top of the list of controversial spouses, as measured by the number of pollster inquiries, is Hillary Clinton during the 1996 campaign, followed by Hillary Clinton during the 1992 campaign, and close behind her is Bill Clinton during the 2016 campaign. As is discussed more thoroughly in the next chapter, many of the pollsters inquires in 1992 revolved around Hillary Clinton's status as a career woman and her interest in having genuine political influence as first lady. Pollsters asked questions such as whether Hillary Clinton was "too pushy," whether she paid "enough attention to her family," and whether she should continue to practice law if she became first lady. In contrast, pollsters only asked basic favorability questions concerning Barbara Bush and whether she made respondents more or less likely to vote for her husband, George H. W. Bush.

In 1996, the high point of polling in this study, the vast majority of questions asked about Hillary Clinton concerned her involvement in the Whitewater real estate investment scandal. Pollsters also questioned the public about whether she was exerting too much influence on Bill Clinton's decisions as president. In contrast, there were only a handful of questions specifically tailored to Elizabeth Dole; however, these questions were clearly prompted by the untraditional aspects of Elizabeth Dole's background and possible political ambitions. One poll, conducted by *The Washington Post*, asked, "Based on what you've seen or heard about Elizabeth Dole during the current presidential campaign, are you more or less likely to vote for her if she were to decide someday to run for president?" (33 percent said more likely, 45 percent less likely). Another poll conducted by *Gallup/CNN/USA Today* asked whether Elizabeth Dole should or should not resume her job as president of the Red Cross if her husband was elected president (75 percent said she should resume her job). The strong level of support for Dole continuing her work is interesting given the mixed feelings the public has about presidential spouses working for pay (Table 2.1). It seems likely that Americans found this idea more palatable because the Red Cross is a non-profit organization dedicated to helping others. Thus, in addition to scandal, pollsters appear concerned with the political and career ambitions of would-be first ladies since having either a career or political ambitions is outside the traditional realm of actions for first ladies.

During the 2000 presidential election cycle, there were a number of polls in response to Tipper Gore's admission that she had suffered from depression (Borman 2003). For example, pollsters asked if her history of depression would make her less qualified to perform the duties of first lady (81 percent said no). Pollsters also asked whether respondents generally shared Tipper Gore's views on warning labels on rock music, homelessness, and mental health issues, reflecting the fact that she had taken high-profile stands on these issues. In contrast, no tailored questions were asked about Laura Bush in 2000, as she was not involved in or outspoken about any controversial public policy issues during the campaign or during the Bush governorship of Texas. Her public actions primarily focused on promoting reading and literacy, having been a librarian in her earlier adult years. Perhaps what is more interesting is that even after being in the public eye as first lady for four years, pollsters still felt no need to ask tailored questions about Laura Bush during the 2004 campaign. Laura Bush's decision to embody a fairly traditional conception of first lady resulted in no controversies for pollsters to query the public about, and very high, approval ratings.

The 2008 and 2012 election cycles also included very few questions beyond the standard favorability survey items. In 2008, there was one question regarding Michelle Obama's statement that this was the first time she was proud of her country, and in 2012 there was a question related to a Democratic strategist's comment about Ann Romney's status as a stay-at-home mom. However, for the most part, neither Michelle Obama, Cindy McCain, nor Ann Romney behaved in ways that sparked political controversy. They followed the script of putting aside their own careers and professional commitments (in the case of Michelle Obama and Cindy McCain) and dutifully and actively campaigned for their spouses while avoiding disputes over major policy controversies.

After Hillary Clinton, Bill Clinton in 2016 was the subject of the most polling inquiries. The bulk of these questions centered on his past sexual transgressions, while three survey items asked about his involvement with the Clinton foundation. Scandals were a centerpiece of the 2016 presidential election contest between Hillary Clinton and Donald Trump, and this focus bled over to public opinion poll questions about their spouses. For Melania Trump, there was one question apiece related to controversies surrounding the publication of nude photos taken during her modeling career, alleged plagiarism in her 2016 Republican Convention Speech, and her immigration history.

Symbolic Representation and Candidate Spouse Evaluations

As the gender gap became a sustained force shaping electoral outcomes, presidential campaigns turned to candidate spouses for the task of appealing to women (Wright 2016). Candidate spouses have embraced this challenge in a variety of ways. A noteworthy example was the "W stands for women" initiative in the 2000 Bush campaign in which Laura Bush participated in events focusing on what the Bush administration would do for women (Carroll 2005; Ferguson 2005; Ferguson and Marso 2007). The convention speeches of presidential candidate spouses, a tradition beginning in the 1990s and becoming an unwritten requirement in the twenty-first century, have all been characterized by a strong emphasis on motherhood and family (Vigil 2014). For example, Ann Romney's 2012 Convention speech focused on the hard work performed by women and mothers and included her shouting out to the audience "I love you women!"

Given that the major party presidential candidate spouses through the 2012 election cycle were all women, as well as the fact that they often make appeals based on issues relating to women, family, and motherhood, there are reasons to think women as a group might feel more favorable than men toward would-be first ladies. The handful of studies exploring public evaluations of first ladies and presidential candidate spouses has examined sex as an independent variable, finding that women sometimes, but not always, feel warmer or more favorable toward candidate spouses relative to men (Burrell et al. 2011; Elder and Frederick 2017; Sulfaro 2007; Knuckey and Kim 2016).

This book goes beyond the previous studies showing that gender shapes political evaluations of presidential candidate spouses, by offering and testing a theory of symbolic representation. This book posits that even though candidate spouses are not on the ballot, they offer important symbolic representation to groups in society whom they represent descriptively and who have historically been marginalized in American politics. Scholars have looked at the concept of symbolic representation along with gender affinity effects in other electoral contexts, such as congressional elections (Dolan 2008) and presidential elections (Simien 2016), and this study extends that research to understanding public evaluations of candidate spouses.

One indication of the symbolic representation of first ladies concerns a question pollsters have repeatedly asked about them: Are they good role models *for women*? This question in and of itself underscores how society and the news media view and assess candidate spouses as symbols of American womanhood. According to polling data archived at the Roper Center for Public Opinion Research across the 1990s, pollsters asked Americans more than a dozen times whether Hillary Clinton was a good role model for *women*, 13 times while she was first lady, twice during the 1992 campaign, and once during the 1996 campaign. This question was also asked of Elizabeth Dole one time during the 1996 presidential election. Interestingly, pollsters never asked whether Barbara Bush or Laura Bush were good role models for women, either during their respective campaigns or while they served as first lady for eight years, perhaps because there was no question that they did in fact represent ideal role models for women. Pollsters returned to this line of questioning once Michelle Obama was poised to become the first lady in December 2008 and asked it again in 2011.

The fact that pollsters asked Americans to assess first ladies and candidate spouses by the standard of whether they are good role models for women is more telling, in many ways, than the actual responses. That said, more Americans responded that Michelle Obama was a good role model for women (in December 2008, 69 percent of Americans responded that Michelle Obama was a good role model for women, and by 2011 this had increased to 73 percent) than Elizabeth Dole (64 percent said Elizabeth Dole was a good role model for women) or Hillary Clinton (responses ranged over time from 59 to 73, but averaged in the low 60s).

In regard to symbolic representation, a particular goal of this study is to determine if groups descriptively represented by first ladies felt closer to candidate spouses than other groups in society. The case study chapters that follow explore the degree to which women, as well as African Americans, and Mormons—also groups that have been marginalized in American politics, especially presidential politics—feel a greater degree of connection with presidential spouses who descriptively represent them. The case study chapters employ multivariate analyses to carefully examine and isolate the role of race, ethnicity, gender, and religion in shaping evaluations of candidate spouses. Here, however, this study draws on survey data to illustrate that women and African Americans do in fact respond to candidate spouses in distinctive ways compared to other groups, thus creating the foundational evidence for this theory of descriptive representation.

Michelle Obama illustrates this phenomenon better than any of the candidate spouses in the time series covered in this book. As shown in greater detail in Chap. 4, both African Americans and women viewed her more favorably even after controlling for key political and demographic variables. In 2011, the *Washington Post* created a survey about Michelle Obama, which provides a particularly good way to understand the role of descriptive representation. This poll not only asked whether respondents thought she was a good role model for women, but also whether respondents personally identified with her, whether Michelle Obama understands the problems of people like you, and whether she shares your values. Results show that women were much more likely than men to say that they personally identified with Michelle Obama (66 percent to 49 percent), and that Michelle Obama understands their problems (74 percent for women versus 64 percent for men).

Of course, Michelle Obama was not only a woman but the first African American first lady. Thus, the issue of race as well as the intersection of race and gender is important to explore. African Americans were much more likely than Whites to feel connected to Michelle Obama and to see her as understanding their problems and values. Also, the *Washington Post* poll asked, “Has having Michelle Obama as the country’s first African American First Lady changed your overall impression of Black women in America, or not?” While most Americans said no, it is interesting that 39 percent of Blacks and 40 percent of Hispanics said yes as compared to 16 percent of Whites, thus once again showing the special importance Michelle Obama held for communities of color. While this survey focused only on Michelle Obama, and lack of survey data prevents a similar analysis on other candidate spouses or first ladies, these statistics support the idea that first ladies have the potential to offer symbolic representation to the groups they descriptively represent.

The survey data collected for this book also lend support to the notion that historically marginalized groups see the position of presidential candidate spouse as particularly important. As discussed earlier in the chapter, 68 percent of respondents feel that during a presidential election it is important or very important for candidate spouses to campaign on behalf of their husbands or wives (Gfk Omni 2017). Multivariate regression analysis of this survey data (not shown here) reveals that this is particularly the case for women and for African Americans. In other words, even after other potentially confounding variables are controlled, women and African Americans were significantly more likely than White respondents or men to feel it is important for candidate spouses to play a visible and active role on the campaign trail. In the case study chapters that follow, we build on this idea, that candidate spouses have the potential to offer meaningful representation to historically marginalized groups and to the groups they descriptively represent, by looking explicitly at the role gender, race, ethnicity, and religion play in shaping public evaluations.

Party Polarization and Candidate Spouses

In addition to understanding why Americans embrace some presidential candidate spouses more than others, as well as the role symbolic representation plays in public evaluations, it is also crucial to understand how the deepening polarization of American politics has or has not affected public perceptions of candidate spouses. In recent decades, the rise of negative partisanship, where partisans express more negative views of political figures in the opposite party, has tended to drive greater polarization in the electorate (Abramowitz and Webster 2016). This trend makes it increasingly difficult for presidential candidate spouses to appeal to voters across party lines.

The case study chapters examining the 1992, 2012, and 2016 elections in more detail, employ multivariate models to examine the role of ideology and partisanship in shaping attitudes toward candidate spouses. Here, to help illustrate the relationship of partisanship and evaluations of presidential candidate spouses over time, Fig. 2.5 plots the partisan gap between Democrats and Republicans (favorable average of Democrats minus favorable average of Republicans) in their evaluations for each election cycle.[4] The party polarization scores for Republicans are negative and thus shown as absolute values to make comparisons across spouses easier.

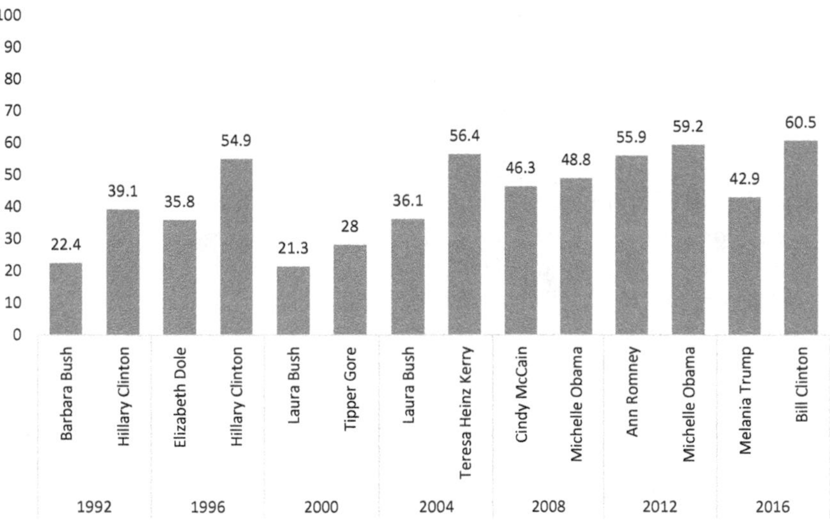

Fig. 2.5 Partisan polarization of attitudes toward presidential candidate spouses

Collectively, what these results show is that just as it does in so many other aspects of political behavior (Campbell et al. 1960; Green et al. 2002; Lewis-Beck et al. 2008), partisanship has a potent impact on how the spouses of presidential candidates have been perceived and received in recent years. In most instances, Democrats and Republicans diverge sharply in their evaluations of these political actors even if they are not on the ballot.

Figure 2.5 also reveals that individual characteristics and actions of the spouses themselves influence just how deep such a divide will materialize. The chart shows that while partisanship is a powerful force in shaping perceptions of candidate spouses, the effects vary, depending on the election cycle. The smallest differential is for Laura Bush in 2000, with Republicans only 21 percentage points more likely to rate her favorably than Democrats. Even after four years in the national spotlight as incumbent first ladies, Barbara Bush in 1992 and Laura Bush in 2004 had relatively low party polarization scores. In contrast, from 1992 through 2006, only Hillary Clinton and Teresa Heinz Kerry had partisan gaps greater than 40 percent. These results suggest that adopting a more traditional approach to the role of presidential spouse minimizes the impact of partisanship.

Another takeaway from this evidence is that partisan polarization in the evaluation of presidential candidate spouses is on an upward trajectory.[5] Starting in 2008, polarization in the 40 plus zone has become standard for evaluations of candidate spouses. Even uncontroversial candidate spouses such as Ann Romney provoked reactions sharply characterized by partisan polarization, suggesting that it is unlikely, if not impossible, for any candidate spouse to reach the levels of popularity once sustained by Barbara Bush and even Laura Bush. Thus, while candidate spouses remain more popular than the presidential candidates in most cases (this issue is discussed more below), they are not immune from rising tide of a public becoming more sharply divided along partisan lines in its evaluation of public figures.

It is also informative to note that a correlation exists between greater polarization and a spouse having lower favorable ratings, but the relationship is not determinative. The 2016 candidate spouses are instructive in this regard. Bill Clinton generated the most polarized reaction of all candidate spouses but was not the least popular spouse. In contrast, Melania Trump was the least popular spouse in the modern era (Figs. 2.2 and 2.3), but evaluations toward her are quite far from being the most polarized. In fact, public evaluations toward Melania Trump are the least polarized since 2004. As Chap. 5 discusses in more depth, the source of Melania Trump's historically low approval ratings is not due to unprecedented levels of partisan polarization.

Spousal Dependence and Independence

The final theoretical lens developed in this book is that of dependence versus independence. To a large degree, perceptions of candidate spouses are shaped by or dependent on perceptions of the spouse/presidential candidate (Elder and Frederick 2017). In fact, individual level analyses of public opinion toward candidate spouses offered in the following chapters show that perceptions of the candidate is the strongest determinant of evaluations toward candidate spouses. At the same time, candidate spouses can and have carved out autonomous personas in the views of many Americans, and are often viewed more favorably than the candidate.

Figure 2.6 shows the net favorable ratings (percent of respondents indicating their evaluation is favorable minus percent indicating their evaluation is unfavorable) for presidential candidates next to the same statistics for their spouses from 1988 through 2016.[6] This analysis sheds light on the similarities and differences in how the public views each presidential candidate and his/her spouse.

Figure 2.6 shows that the views of presidential spouses are correlated, but are not determinatively so. The correlation between the two variables is 0.289, showing that the relationship is positive but not statistically significant at the 0.05 level. In fact, Fig. 2.6 reveals that there is sometimes a sizable gap in how the public views presidential candidates and how they view their spouses. In 1988, for example, more people had unfavorable than favorable views of Michel Dukakis, yet the public had very positive views of his wife, Kitty Dukakis. Similarly, while evaluations of Barbara Bush were certainly shaped by the way the public viewed her husband (as shown in the next chapter), she enjoyed dramatically greater popularity than George H. W. Bush did. The gap between views of Barbara Bush and George H. W. Bush in 1992 is the biggest in the time series, and it vividly illustrates the concept of independence.

While perceptions of candidates and their spouses are not always as dramatically different as in these two cases, there is a difference in each case, typically showing that spouses are usually, although not always, more popular than their presidential candidate spouse. One explanation for this is that Americans have empathy for candidate spouses since they do not

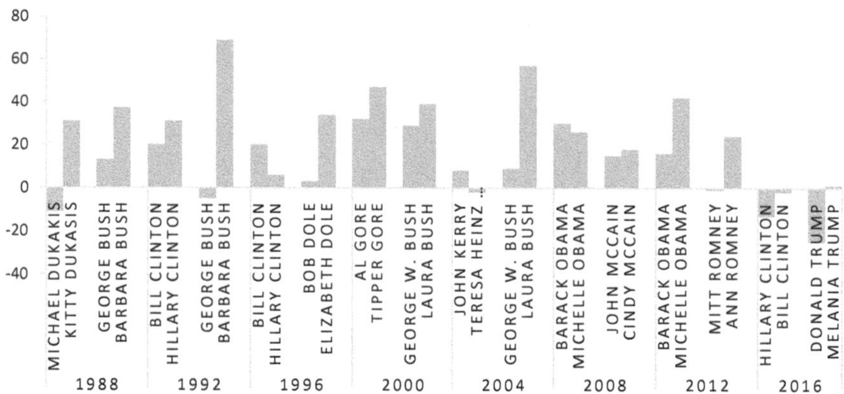

Fig. 2.6 "Independence"—net favorable ratings of presidential candidates and their spouses

choose the public spotlight but rather are thrust into it due to the political ambitions of their spouses. In fact, original survey data collected in 2017 reveal that a significant minority of Americans, 23 percent, believe that presidential candidate spouses should be viewed with more sympathy than other political figures who campaign on behalf of presidential candidates, a view held equally by Republicans and Democrats (Gfk Omni 2017). The reserve of warmth and empathy that about a quarter of Americans have for candidate spouses may explain their ability to maintain images that are to some degree autonomous and often more favorable than the candidates themselves.

The media often refers to spouses as the presidential candidate's secret weapon, a reference to their wide and strong appeal, yet in a small number of cases the candidate himself is more popular. The three exceptions to this general rule of spouses being more popular than the candidates are the Clintons in 1996 when Bill Clinton's favorable average was a little higher than Hillary Clinton's, the Kerry's in 2004, and interestingly the Obamas in 2008 (although the difference was small and both were quite popular). Thus, while some Americans may in general have greater sympathy for candidate spouses than other national political figures, this sympathy only appears to flow to candidate spouses who operate within the traditional expectations for candidate spouses and not to those would-be first ladies such as Teresa Heinz Kerry or Hillary Clinton who challenge traditional expectations in their presentation and actions. The case study chapters that follow explore in more detail the degree to which the views of the candidates shape views of the spouse, as well as how and why candidate spouses are able to maintain images separate from that of their spouses.

Conclusion

This chapter demonstrates that expectations for candidate spouses remain traditional, but at the same time the public has come to expect spouses to be visible and active on the campaign trail, a set of expectations that can be referred to as new traditionalism. Spouses that are able and willing to project an image corresponding to new traditionalism tend to be more popular, while those spouses who cultivate a profile that in some significant way deviates from these norms tend to be less popular. Indeed, incumbent first ladies only appear to accrue incumbency advantage when they perform in line with the expectations of new traditionalism as did Barbara Bush, Laura Bush, and Michelle Obama. To do otherwise is to provoke public concern, reflected in lower approval ratings and an increase in the number of tailored polling inquiries made, as was the case with Hillary Clinton.

Beyond new traditionalism, this chapter explored data showing that first ladies resonate with groups they represent descriptively, an idea explored further in the coming chapters in relation to all candidate spouses, not just first ladies. Finally, this chapter shows that while partisanship and spouse evaluations do shape the public's perceptions of the wives and husband of presidential candidates, the candidate spouses are able, to some degree, to rise above and carve out an autonomous image. The next three chapters apply these theoretical frameworks to better understand public opinion toward the diverse set of presidential candidate spouses featured in the 1992, 2012, and 2016 elections.

Notes

1. Of course, Hillary Clinton did not continue her career as first lady during her time in the White House, but much of the political discourse at the time centered on how she embraced feminist ideals and how she had continued her career as a lawyer while her husband held political office in Arkansas. During the 1992 campaign, she made it clear she would draw on her wealth of career experiences to play an active role as a key policy adviser to President Bill Clinton (Troy 2006).

2. The survey was conducted using the web-enabled KnowledgePanel®, a probability-based panel designed to be representative of the US population. Initially, participants are chosen scientifically by a random selection of telephone numbers and residential addresses. Persons in selected households are then invited by telephone or by mail to participate in the web-enabled KnowledgePanel®. For those who agree to participate, but do not already have Internet access, GfK provides at no cost a laptop and ISP connection. People who already have computers and Internet service are permitted to participate using their own equipment. Panelists then receive unique log-in information for accessing surveys online, and then are sent emails throughout each month inviting them to participate in research. The sample for each wave's KP OmniWeb consists of 1000 completed interviews, made up of male and female adults (in approximately equal number), all 18 years of age and over. All completed interviews are weighted to ensure accurate and reliable representation of the total population, 18 years and older.
3. The percentage unable to rate each spouse is not explicitly shown in Fig. 2.1. Elizabeth Dole had the second-highest percentage of respondents unable to rate her at 45 percent, followed by Teresa Heinz Kerry at 44 percent.
4. These scores were calculated using data sets archived at the Roper Center for Public Opinion Research. The available data set closest to the election for each presidential campaign was used.
5. This chart likely understates the level of partisan polarization in evaluations of presidential candidate spouses since it excludes the 1988 election for which we lack data. It is reasonable to speculate that partisanship was probably much less of factor in assessments of Barbara Bush and Kitty Dukakis.
6. Data are drawn from a national opinion poll archived at the Roper Center for Public Opinion Research close to the election. We use the net favorability rating for both the candidates and the spouses since fewer respondents have an opinion about the spouse.

Bibliography

Abramowitz, Alan I., and Stephen Webster. 2016. The Rise of Negative Partisanship and the Nationalization of U.S. Elections in the 21st Century. *Electoral Studies* 41 (1): 12–22.

Ansolabehere, Stephen, and James M. Snyder Jr. 2004. The Incumbency Advantage in U.S. Elections: An Analysis of State and Federal Offices, 1942–2000. *Election Law Journal: Rules, Politics, and Policy* 1 (15): 315–338.

Benze, James G., Jr. 1990. Nancy Reagan: China Doll or Dragon Lady? *Presidential Studies Quarterly* 20 (4): 777–790.

Borman, Jan. 2003. Depression in Women's Magazines. *Journal of the American Psychiatric Nurses Association* 9 (3): 71–76.

Borrelli, Maryanne. 2001. Competing Conceptions of the First Ladyship: Public Responses to Betty Ford's 60 Minutes Interview. *Presidential Studies Quarterly* 31: 397–414.

Burrell, Barbara. 1999. The Governmental Status of the First Lady in Law and in Public Perception. In *Women in Politics: Outsiders or Insiders?* ed. Lois Duke Whitaker, 233–247. Upper Saddle River, NJ: Prentice Hall.

———. 2000. Hillary Rodham Clinton as First Lady: The People's Perspective. *The Social Science Journal* 37 (4): 529–546.

Burrell, Barbara, Laurel Elder, and Brian Frederick. 2011. From Hillary to Michelle: Public Opinion and the Spouses of Presidential Candidates. *Presidential Studies Quarterly* 41 (1): 156–176.

Campbell, Angus, Phillip E. Converse, Warren E. Miller, and Donald E. Stokes. 1960. *The American Voter*. Chicago, IL: University of Chicago Press.

Caroli, Betty Boyd. 2010. *First Ladies: From Martha Washington to Michelle Obama*. Oxford: Oxford University.

Carroll, Susan J. 2005. Voter Choices: Meet You at the Gender Gap. In *Gender and Elections: Shaping the Future of American Politics*, ed. Susan J. Carroll and Richard L. Fox. Cambridge: Cambridge University Press.

Dolan, Kathleen. 2008. Is There a "Gender Affinity Effect" in American Politics? Information, Affect and Candidate Sex in U.S. House Elections. *Political Research Quarterly* 61 (1): 79–89.

Dowd, Maureen. 2004. The Doctor is Out. *New York Times*, January 15.

Dubriwny, Tasha W. 2005. First Ladies and Feminism: Laura Bush as Advocate for Women's and Children's Rights. *Women's Studies in Communications* 28 (1): 84–114.

Elder, Laurel, and Brian Frederick. 2017. Perceptions of Candidate Spouses in the 2012 Presidential Election: The Role of Gender, Race, Religion, and Partisanship. *Politics, Groups, and Identities*. https://doi.org/10.1080/21565503.2017.1338969

Ferguson, Michaele L. 2005. 'W' Stands for Women: Feminism and Security Rhetoric in the Post 9/11 Bush Administration. *Politics & Gender* 1 (1): 9–38.

Ferguson, Michaele L., and Lori Jo Marso, eds. 2007. *W Stands for Women: How the George W. Bush Presidency Shaped a New Politics of Gender*. Durham, NC: Duke University Press.

Gallup/USA Today Poll, September, 2004 [survey question]. USGALLUP.04SEP T013.R35F. Gallup Organization [producer]. Cornell University, Ithaca, NY: Roper Center for Public Opinion Research, iPOLL [distributor]. Accessed August 10, 2017.

Gfk Omni Survey. 2017. KnowledgePanel (KP) OmniWeb Survey Conducted by Gfk Custom Research LLC, September 15–17.

Green, Donald P., Bradley Palmquist, and Eric Schickler. 2002. *Partisan Hearts and Minds: Political Parties and the Social Identities of Voters*. New Haven, CT: Yale University Press.

Jacobson, Gary C., and Jamie L. Carson. 2015. *The Politics of Congressional Elections*. 9th ed. Lanham, MD: Rowman and Littlefield.

Knuckey, Jonathan, and Myunghee Kim. 2016. Evaluations of Michelle Obama as First Lady: The Role Racial Resentment. *Presidential Studies Quarterly* 46 (2): 365–386.

Lewis-Beck, Michael S., William G. Jacoby, Helmut Norpoth, and Herbert F. Weisberg. 2008. *The American Voter Revisited*. Ann Arbor, MI: University of Michigan Press.

Mandziuk, Roseann M. 2017. Whither the Good Wife? 2016 Presidential Candidate Spouses in the Gendered Spaces of Contemporary Politics. *Quarterly Journal of Speech* 103 (1–2): 136–159. https://doi.org/10.1080/00335630.2016.1233350.

Mayhew, David R. 2008. Incumbency Advantage in U.S. Presidential Elections: The Historical Record. *Presidential Studies Quarterly* 123 (2): 201–228.

Rhodan, Maya. 2016. Hillary Clinton Says Bill Clinton Would Be in Charge of the Economy After Election. *Time*, May 16.

Saad, Lydia. 2017. Gallup Vault: A See Change in Support for Working Women. *Gallup*, July 20.

Shoop, Tiffany J. 2010. From Professionals to Potential First Ladies: How Newspapers Told the Stories of Cindy McCain and Michelle Obama. *Sex Roles* 63: 807–819.

Simien, Evelyn M. 2016. *Historic Firsts: How Symbolic Empowerment Changes U.S. Politics*. New York: Oxford University Press.

Stokes, Ashli Quesinberry. 2005. First Ladies in Waiting: The Fight for Rhetorical Legitimacy on the Campaign Trail. In *The 2004 Presidential Campaign: A Communication Perspective*, ed. Robert J. Denton. Lanham, MD: Rowman & Littlefield.

Sulfaro, Valerie. 2007. Affective Evaluations of First Ladies: A Comparison of Hillary Clinton and Laura Bush. *Presidential Studies Quarterly* 37: 486–514.

Thurman, Judith. 2004. The Candidate's Wife: Teresa Heinz Kerry is an Uncharted Element on the Road to the White House. *The New Yorker*, September 27.

Tien, Charles, Regan Checchio, and Arthur H. Miller. 1999. The Impact of First Wives on Presidential Campaigns and Elections. In *Women in Politics: Outsiders or Insiders?* ed. Lois Duke Whitaker, 149–168. Upper Saddle River, NJ: Prentice Hall.

Troy, Gil. 2006. *Hillary Clinton: Polarizing First Lady*. Lawrence, KS: Kansas University Press.

Vigil, Tammy R. 2014. Feminine Views in the Feminine Style: Convention Speeches by Presidential Nominees' Spouses. *Southern Communication Journal* 79: 327–346.

Washington Post. 2011. Kaiser/Washington Post Black Women in America Survey, Oct, 2011 [survey question]. USSSRS.2011WPH029.Q11A. Social Science Research Solutions [producer]. Cornell University, Ithaca, NY: Roper Center for Public Opinion Research, iPOLL [distributor]. Accessed August 18, 2017.

Wright, Lauren. 2016. *On Behalf of the President: Presidential Spouses and White House Communications Strategy Today*. Praeger.

CHAPTER 3

Hillary Clinton Versus Barbara Bush: Tradition Meets Change in the 1992 Presidential Campaign

Hillary Rodham Clinton and Barbara Bush represented strikingly distinctive portrayals and perspectives on how they viewed the role of first lady in their husbands' 1992 campaigns for president, presentations that would spark reactions from the American public that varied quite dramatically. Barbara Bush was considerably older than Hillary Clinton, 67 years old compared to 44 years in 1992. Barbara Bush had not pursued a professional career, but rather devoted her time to raising her children and supporting her husband's political career. She came to the 1992 campaign, having spent the prior four years as a very popular first lady embracing the traditional role of the president's spouse. During her first ladyship, she adopted the cause of literacy, a non-controversial issue, and was little involved in Bush administration policy-making. Her 1992 Republican National Convention speech, which marked the first time a presidential candidate's spouse gave a prime-time address, focused almost exclusively on traditionally feminine themes such as families and being a champion of her husband, President George H. W. Bush (Vigil 2014).

Hillary Clinton, on the other hand, graduated from Yale University Law School, worked with Marian Wright Edelman's Children's Defense Fund, served as a legal counsel member of the President Nixon impeachment inquiry staff, and had been named one of the nation's top 100 lawyers by the *National Journal* (Burrell 2001, 25; Ifill 1992; Troy 2006). She was one of only two female faculty members in the School of Law at the University of Arkansas, Fayetteville, after she married Bill Clinton and

L. Elder et al., *American Presidential Candidate Spouses*,
https://doi.org/10.1007/978-3-319-73879-6_3

moved to that state. Bill Clinton was elected governor in 1978, lost his re-election bid in 1980, and regained the governorship in 1982. Throughout Bill Clinton's tenure as governor of Arkansas, Hillary Clinton served as his political and policy-making partner while working as a partner in the Rose Law firm in Little Rock (Burrell 2001, 25; Troy 2006). She did not take her husband's name until she was advised that her use of her maiden name may hurt her husband's political career (Ifill 1992). Early in the 1992 presidential election, the Clintons initiated and encouraged the idea that Hillary would be a vital political adviser in the White House and would play a prominent role in a Clinton presidency (Burrell 2001, 25). The aspiring president explained that if he were elected, "it would be an unprecedented partnership, far more than Franklin Roosevelt and Eleanor" (Sheehy 1992, 144). As Barbara Burrell describes in her book on Hillary Clinton, during the 1992 presidential campaign, the Clintons "promoted the notion of a dramatically different partnership to lead the country" (2001, 26).

This chapter analyzes public perceptions of the 1992 presidential candidate spouses, Hillary Clinton and Barbara Bush, paying particular attention to how pollsters and the public responded as these two women conformed to and challenged traditional expectations for the role of would-be first lady. By serving as a highly visible campaign surrogate while embracing a traditional role that avoided mention of any major policy influence, Barbara Bush in many ways pioneered the concept of new traditionalism discussed in the previous chapter. Hillary Clinton was also active on the campaign trail, but was much less traditional in her role as presidential candidate spouse, by highlighting her own professional accomplishments and promising to play a significant policy role in a Bill Clinton White House. Drawing on the framework of symbolic representation, this chapter explores the way specific groups in the electorate including women and those with feminist leanings viewed these two presidential candidate spouses. This chapter also looks more deeply at the ways partisanship, ideology, and perceptions of the presidential candidates shaped the public's view of these women.

Barbara Bush on the Campaign Trail in 1992

Barbara Bush was an ever present and formidable campaigner for her husband, President George H. W. Bush in his bid for re-election 1992. She visited well over 300 cities campaigning for her husband (Keen 1992).

Indeed, she provided key testimony on behalf of his qualifications to be re-elected and was considered "a formable campaign weapon." "Everyone loves Barbara" was a popular quote in the media during this election campaign. Supporters even created "Re-elect Barbara's Husband in '92" buttons. George H. W. Bush was struggling in his re-election bid. The lagging economy in particular was hurting his chances for re-election, and thus Barbara Bush's presence on the campaign trail was significant because of her high popularity and the popular perceptions of her. She was considered his "number 1 surrogate."

Barbara Bush's likability factor, as evidenced in the public opinion data presented in Chap. 2, was key to her importance to the campaign. "[N]obody is better-credentialed to talk about the human being that George Bush is than Barbara Bush. She reminds people how much they like the Bushes. And that is an important ingredient in reminding them how to vote," commented Sheila Tate, Bush's press secretary in his 1988 campaign (Radcliffe 1992). Democratic political analyst Celinda Lake, too, noted Barbara Bush as being essential to her husband's image. "The strongest part of Bush's domestic issues is being supportive of family values. She is key to that. He has very little credibility now, so he says, 'Barbara and I care'" (Radcliffe 1992).

An *Associated Press* headline early in the campaign season underscores her importance to the campaign. "Bush, Launching Campaign, Takes a Ride on First Lady's Popularity" headlined a Harry Rosenthal piece.

> With a whole firmament of politicians to choose from, George Bush tapped his wife Barbara to introduce his reelection announcement Wednesday. Small wonder: She's the popular one in the First Family... Wherever they go, she gets the warmest reception, a fact not lost on Bush, who invokes her name more and more as his own ratings sink. Some say he is riding her coattails at a time when he needs all the help he can get (1992).

Barbara Bush's emphasis as she campaigned was in the mode of the traditional lady for the most part. "She still jokes about her hair and her age; still evokes her grandmotherly credentials; still insists her political instincts are" about zero; "still calls George Bush" by far the best qualified "candidate to lead this country; still claims she doesn't talk about issues; and still uses some of the same lines she used before" (Radcliffe 1992). She was introduced as "America's mom" at campaign stops (Monastra 1992). She and other female family members traveled on the "Bush Family Express '92." Her speech at the 1992 Republican Convention, the first time a presidential candidate spouse gave a prime-time speech, emphasized the importance of family as its central theme (Vigil 2014). She highlighted her experiences as a stay-at-home mom, serving as a den mother, and going to countless little league games, and she emphasized that at the top of her husband's accomplishments was that he was a wonderful father. As Caroli (2010) points out, Barbara Bush was voted most admired woman in America four years in a row by readers of *Good Housekeeping* magazine. This support suggests her message and persona appealed to many women who did not pursue careers outside the home.

Toward the final stages of the campaign, with George Bush lagging in the polls, issues did take on a larger role in her remarks. She would tick off the president's accomplishments and criticized Congress for not being supportive (Keen 1992). Her policy-oriented remarks were in support of her husband's work, rather than expressing any interest of her own to influence policy or shape his decisions. In summary, in 1992, Barbara Bush brought the role of the candidate spouse to new heights and importance (Mughan and Burden 1995) while maintaining a traditional image, emphasizing her role as a mother and supporter of her husband, and in this way she pioneered the notion of new traditionalism.

Hillary Clinton Challenges Tradition on the Campaign Trail

Although Hillary Clinton did not give an address at the 1992 Democratic Convention (Vigil 2014), she, like Barbara Bush, was very active in her husband's campaign for president. Hillary Clinton traveled across the country headlining events on behalf of her husband and fielded hundreds of interview requests; she was viewed by most as a prime strategist in her husband's campaign (Ifill 1992). The themes and issues Hillary Clinton emphasized in her campaign appearances were women, children, and the workforce; she said that making progress on these issues was what most motivated her to be involved in her husband's campaign (Ifill 1992). While some candidate wives acted as surrogates for their husbands prior to the 1990s,[1] the active roles of both Barbara Bush and Hillary Clinton illustrate that the 1992 election was a break with the past in terms of the importance and visibility of would-be first ladies (Burrell 2001; Mughan and Burden 1995).

In contrast to the traditional role embraced by Barbara Bush, the Clintons made it clear that if Bill Clinton was elected, then Hillary Clinton would be involved in shaping policy and influencing decisions. Bill Clinton encouraged speculation that Hillary Clinton would be appointed to a Cabinet post (Burrell 2001, 25). At fundraisers, Bill Clinton would quip "Buy one, get one free" (Burrell 2001, 25). And on the campaign trail, Hillary Clinton would state that "If you elect Bill, you get me" (Burrell 2001, 25).

Hillary Clinton's role and performance in the 1992 election campaign presented in stark relief the challenge of contemporary feminism to the traditional idea of a first lady. Clinton herself stimulated much of the debate with her Tammy Wynette comment in a *60 Minutes* interview early in the campaign season that "I am not sitting here, some little woman standing by her man like Tammy Wynette" (in reference to Bill Clinton's reputation as a philanderer). Similarly in response to a reporter's question on the campaign trail, Hillary Clinton commented that "I suppose I could have stayed home and baked cookies and had teas, but what I decided to do was to fulfill my profession" (Burrell 2001, 31).

News stories discussed the contradictions and challenges emanating from Clinton's participation in the election. For example, the *New York Times* referenced her as "a lightning rod for the mixed emotions we have about work and motherhood, dreams and accommodation, smart women and men's worlds" (Quindlen 1992), and the *Los Angeles Times* commented that "[t]he squirming over Hillary Clinton isn't so much about a first lady as about ambivalence over women, power, work and marriage" (Morrison 1992). Jacklyn Friedman writing in the *American Prospect* sharply described the conundrum of female spouses moving from traditional to what we might call a "modern" first lady in keeping with women's quests for equality.

> That election was a watershed year for redefining the role of the potential president's wife, in part because we'd never seen a potential First Lady like Hillary before. She was a Rorschach test for a country still rearranging itself in the wake of the feminist second wave, and no one—not even the Clintons—understood which rules could be changed, and which were still third rails of gender performance. How could it not be confusing? Even in Arkansas, even in the '80s, Hillary Clinton was able to practice law while her husband governed, a scenario that became so threatening when translated to a run for the White House it gave rise to the now-traditional First Lady Bake-Off. (2012)

Hillary Clinton's uniquely prominent and untraditional role in the 1992 presidential campaign spurred innumerable news stories and dozens of inquiries from pollsters. She was the object of press scrutiny during the 1992 campaign to an extent not faced by any previous contemporary would-be first lady. As reporter Matthew Cooper wrote at the time, "She engendered spirited public debate" (Cooper 1992). Headlines such as "The Hillary Factor," "The Hillary Problem," "All Eyes on Hillary," and "Hillary Then and Now" were typical of news headlines during the campaign (Burrell 2001, 26).

Hillary Clinton's untraditional role also fueled political opponents to attack her to an extent candidate wives had seldom, if ever, experienced. "Hillary-bashing" was common on the campaign trail (Burrell 2001, 30–31). At the Republican National Convention in Houston, multiple speakers infused their speeches with negative remarks toward Hillary Clinton prompting one observer to contend that "Hillary-bashing became the order of the day" in a way few presidential candidate spouses had ever had to deal with on such a national stage (Troy 2006, 54). During her speech, wife of the Republican vice-presidential candidate Marilyn Quayle criticized Hillary Clinton for implying that family was oppressive and women could only thrive apart from it, and went on to state that "most women do not want to be liberated from their essential natures as women. Most of us love being mothers and wives" (Burrell 2001, 31).

Attitudes Toward Hillary Clinton and Barbara Bush over the 1992 Campaign Season

To understand the public's response to the strikingly different portrayals of would-be first ladies Barbara Bush and Hillary Clinton offered, this chapter presents public opinion polls about Barbara Bush and Hillary Clinton over the course of the 1992 campaign. Figures 3.1 and 3.2 draw on polls archived at the Roper Center for Public Opinion Research to plot the favorable and unfavorable ratings of the two candidate spouses from January 1992 through the election.

As discussed in the previous chapter, Barbara Bush remains the most popular first lady in contemporary times. She has been described as "the First Lady that most voters know only as a kindly, snowy-haired grandmother" (Stanley 1992). As Fig. 3.1 shows, few people disliked Barbara Bush across the campaign season, despite her playing a high-profile role in

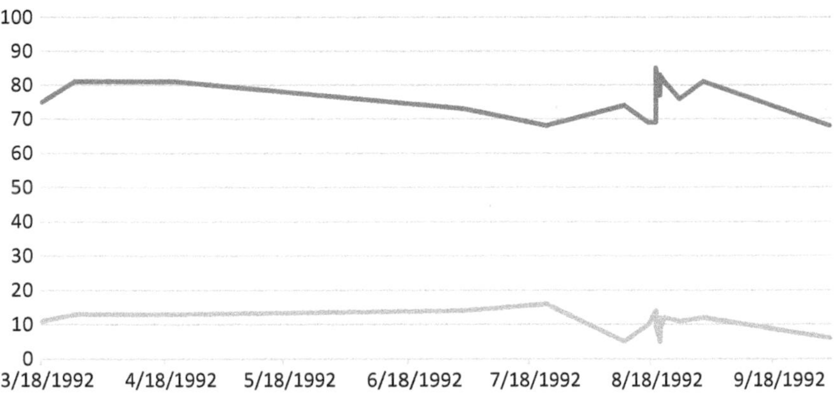

Fig. 3.1 Barbara Bush's favorable/unfavorable ratings across the 1992 campaign

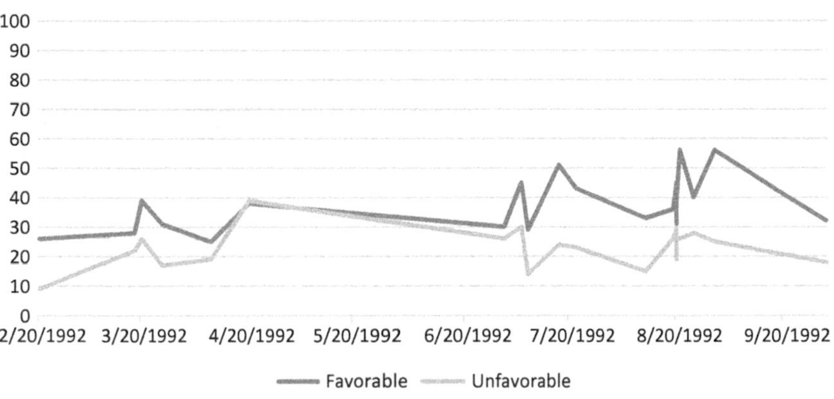

Fig. 3.2 Hillary Clinton's favorable/unfavorable ratings across the 1992 campaign

her husband's campaign, a role that could potentially have politicized views of her. Her unfavorable ratings peaked at 16 percent in July of 1992 and were typically lower. Her favorable ratings remained in the 1970s or even the 1980s across the campaign season.

The incumbency advantage of serving as sitting first lady explains some, but not all, of Barbara Bush's immense popularity. As Chap. 2 documents, Barbara Bush was also very popular in 1988, with an 81 percent adjusted favorable rating compared to 79 percent for Kitty Dukakis. Clearly 1988 was a different period in presidential elections when candidate spouses were well received by most Americans, regardless of party. That said, through her traditional performance, Barbara Bush benefited from the platform of being first lady. Across her four years in the national spotlight, she focused on literacy and family, she remained steadfast as a champion of her husband, and as a result she became even more beloved, increasing her adjusted favorable rating seven percentage points, from 1988 to 1992, to a remarkable 88 percent.

As the incumbent first lady in the 1992 election, Barbara Bush was far more familiar to the general public than Hillary Clinton. Even given the attention-grabbing headlines about Hillary Clinton early in the campaign, fewer people were able to offer an assessment of Hillary Clinton for much of the campaign season than for Barbara Bush, although polls did show an unusually fast decline in respondents expressing “no opinion” (Burrell 2001). Figure 3.2 shows that among those respondents having an opinion of Hillary Clinton, negative views of her rose and then fell as the campaign progressed. In dramatic contrast to Barbara Bush, views of Hillary Clinton were quite polarized, with unfavorable views almost as high as favorable views. As shown in Chap. 2, Hillary Clinton’s adjusted favorable average, at 55 percent, was much lower than that of Barbara Bush’s adjusted favorable average in either 1988 when it was 81 percent, or 1992 when it was 88 percent. It is clear that Hillary Clinton’s decision to buck the traditional role of candidate spouse resulted in less favorable and more polarized views of her.

Pollster Inquiries

While Barbara Bush was much better known to the American public, Hillary Clinton was the source of much more media and pollster attention across the campaign because she challenged rather than conformed to traditional expectations for presidential spouses. Not only had Hillary Clinton continued to pursue her legal career while her husband was governor of Arkansas, rather than devoting herself to motherhood and supporting her husband in a behind-the-scenes manner, but also Hillary Clinton and her husband were explicit about her intention to act as a political and policy adviser in the White House (Table 3.1).

Based on a poll questions archived at the Roper Center for Public Opinion Research from January 1, 1992, through election day, November 4, 60 survey items queried about Hillary Clinton, while only 19 asked about Barbara

Table 3.1 Pollster inquiries about presidential candidate spouses during the 1992 campaign season

Poll questions asked about Barbara Bush, 22

Favorability type questions (19): For example,

- Is your opinion of Barbara Bush favorable, not favorable, undecided, or haven't you heard enough about Barbara Bush yet to have an opinion?

Tailored questions (3):

- Does Barbara Bush help or hurt George Bush's chance for election in November?
- Have Barbara Bush's actions and statements made you more or less likely to vote for President Bush for re-election?
- Does Barbara Bush make you more/less likely to vote for her husband?

Poll questions asked about Hilary Clinton, 60

Favorability type questions (26): For example,

- Is your opinion of Hillary Clinton favorable, not favorable, undecided, or haven't you heard enough about Hillary Clinton yet to have an opinion?

Tailored questions (34): For example,

- Does your opinion of Hillary make you more/less likely to vote for her husband, Bill Clinton? (5)
- Policy and advising role (e.g. Should she shape policy, work in cabinet/as adviser?) (6)
- Political ambition (e.g. Could she be president, would she make better president, is she too ambitious to be good first lady?) (4)
- Republican criticism of Hillary (e.g. Do you agree? Are criticisms fair?) (6)
- Role model and gender roles (e.g. Is she a positive role model? Does she pay enough attention to her family? Is she too pushy? Is she someone you admire?) (9)
- First lady (e.g. should she continue to practice law? Be traditional first lady?) (4)

Source: Polls archived at the Roper Center for Public Opinion Research from January 1, 1992, through election day, November 4, 1992

Bush. As Table 2.2 in Chap. 2 shows, the media polls about Barbara Bush focused almost exclusively on measuring respondents' favorability toward her. The handful of tailored questions asked about her were relatively benign, focusing on whether Barbara Bush helped or hurt her husband's chances for re-election. Not surprisingly, given her popularity, a large majority of Americans (79 percent) felt she helped his chances (*U.S. News & World Report* Poll 1992).

In dramatic contrast, the public was asked about a variety of aspects of a potential Hillary Clinton first ladyship. National samples were asked whether she should shape policy and work in the cabinet as an adviser to the president. Respondents were asked about her political ambition, whether she was a positive role model, did she pay enough attention to her family, was she too pushy, and should she continue to practice law or be a traditional first lady. The fact that pollsters asked these types of questions about Hillary Clinton and not Barbara Bush reveals how Hillary Clinton's untraditional presentation as a candidate spouse was jarring to much of society. Responses to these questions also reveal Americans' uneasiness with a politically active first lady, as discussed in the previous chapter. For example, a survey from April 1992 revealed that 60 percent of Americans were opposed to the idea of Hillary Clinton serving in the Cabinet, while only 25 percent favored this idea (*U.S. News & World Report* Poll 1992). Overall, the number and substance of pollster inquiries about candidate spouses across the 1992 campaign are reflective of the way that Barbara Bush conformed to traditional expectations while Hillary Clinton challenged traditional expectations of candidate spouses.

Individual-Level Analyses

For the first time in their series of election studies, the 1992 ANES included the potential first ladies in its "feeling thermometer" questions about political leaders and other people in the news, a decision reflecting the more visible and important role candidate spouses played in the 1992 election compared to previous years.

This section of the chapter draws on the 1992 ANES data set to further our understanding of public opinion toward the 1992 presidential candidate spouses.

Instead of presenting respondents with a binary choice of whether they have a favorable or unfavorable view of the spouse, the ANES asks respondents to evaluate individuals on a continuous scale, from 0 being the most negative value, to 100 being the most positive, with 50 indicating a neutral response. The ANES also includes a rich array of demographic, political, and attitudinal variables, which allow for a robust exploration of the individual-level factors shaping attitudes toward candidate spouses. This chapter and the next two chapters explore the role of key demographic variables including gender, race, ethnicity, age, and White Evangelical status in shaping attitudes toward presidential candidate spouses because these variables are key determinants of political attitudes and evaluations and because some of these variables are critical to assessing our theoretical framework of symbolic representation. Each chapter also explores the relationship between evaluations of the spouses and political variables relating to our theoretical frameworks including partisanship, ideology, and evaluations of the candidates. When data permit, analyses include other relevant attitudinal variables including attitudes toward feminism, Africans Americans, and Mormons.

This chapter and the two following case study chapters present two types of analyses. The first is bivariate relationships between key independent variables and the feeling thermometer averages of the presidential candidate spouses, in this case, Barbara Bush and Hillary Clinton. Figure 3.3 presents the mean thermometer rating averages of Hillary Clinton and Barbara Bush for various demographic and political groups. Second, the chapter presents two sets of multivariate results, one predicting feelings toward Barbara Bush (Table 3.2) and one predicting feelings toward Hillary Clinton (Table 3.3). Three different versions of each model are presented to address the problem that several independent variables are correlated with one another. One model includes all relevant independent variables. The second model excludes partisanship and ideology. The third model excludes the ratings of the presidential candidates.

The bivariate and multivariate analyses allow for a deeper exploration of questions raised in the first half of the chapter. To what extent do partisanship and ideology account for the American publics' comparatively less positive embrace of Hillary Clinton and to what extent did Barbara Bush's traditional approach to being a presidential spouse allow her to rise above partisan and ideological polarization? Given that Hillary Clinton and Barbara Bush were not only two of the most visible women involved in the

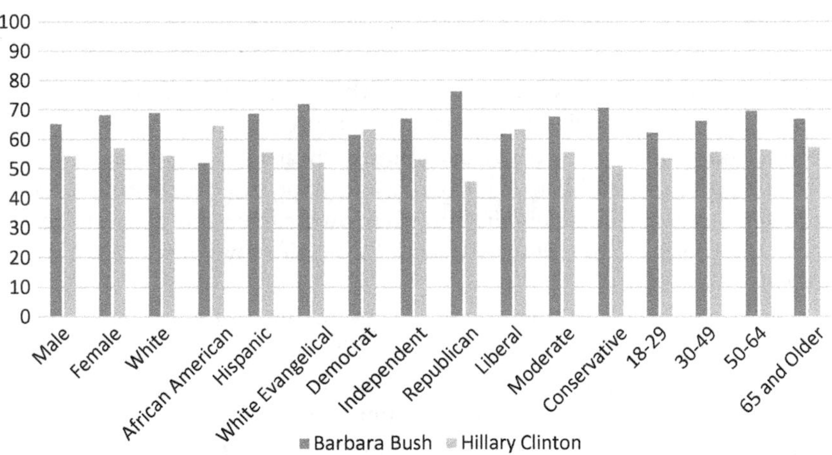

Fig. 3.3 Mean feeling thermometer ratings of Barbara Bush and Hillary Clinton among demographic and political groups from 1992 ANES

Table 3.2 Regression models predicting respondents' feeling thermometer rating of Barbara Bush in the 1992 election

Independent variable	*Model 1*	*Model 2*	*Model 3*
Demographics			
Age	0.197* (0.037)	0.187* (0.032)	0.194* (0.042)
Education	1.193* (0.401)	1.408* (0.368)	0.870* (0.459)
Income	0.373* (0.113)	0.345* (0.099)	0.518* (0.130)
Black	−7.378* (2.311)	−8.597* (6.390)	6.437* (2.649)
Hispanic	−14.778* (6.812)	−12.491* (6.390)	−11.485 (7.797)
Female	4.832* (1.210)	4.367* (1.082)	5.178* (1.387)
Born Again Evangelical	2.537 (1.478)	1.880 (1.314)	4.205* (1.691)
Political variables			
Party ID (more Republican)	−0.084 (0.430)		3.032* (0.421)
Ideology (more conservative)	0.255 (0.532)		2.028* (0.596)
Feeling thermometers			
Hillary Clinton	0.130* (0.038)	150* (0.035)	0.070 (0.037)
George Bush	0.428* (0.029)	0.450* (0.022)	
Bill Clinton	−0.118* (0.038)	−0.086* (0.033)	
Feminists	−0.009 (0.032)	−0.031 (0.028)	−0.052 (0.036)
Constant	23.137* (4.635)	21.150* (3.501)	
Adjusted R^2	0.429	0.420	0.248
N	755	987	756

Note: Parameter estimates are unstandardized regression coefficients with standard errors in parentheses. Data are from the 1992 ANES

$^*p < 0.05$

1992 campaign, but also spoke about the experiences of women and appealed to women, did women view them more favorably than men, suggesting that women felt a particular affinity toward the candidate spouses? Similarly, given that Hillary Clinton was arguably the first feminist presidential candidate spouse highlighting her own career and desire to influence policy in the White House, how did attitudes toward feminism shape attitudes toward her?

The basic feeling thermometer ratings of Barbara Bush and Hillary Clinton from the 1992 ANES confirm the aggregate poll results discussed previously, showing that Barbara Bush was viewed very favorably by the public, with an average feeling thermometer rating of 67. In comparison, the public viewed Hillary Clinton less favorably, giving her an average feeling thermometer rating of 56. Looking at the dispersion of their ANES feeling thermometer ratings is also instructive, revealing that

Table 3.3 Regression models predicting respondents' feeling thermometer rating of Hillary Clinton in the 1992 election

Independent variable	*Model 1*	*Model 2*	*Model 3*
Demographics			
Age	0.008 (0.035)	0.013 (0.029)	0.057 (0.042)
Education	0.164 (0.383)	0.106 (0.332)	0.025 (0.454)
Income	0.044 (0.108)	0.038 (0.089)	−0.024 (0.129)
Black	3.371 (2.202)	1.559 (1.709)	5.366* (2.619)
Hispanic	3.724 (6.476)	1.239 (5.740)	11.759 (7.700)
Female	1.089 (1.158)	0.796 (0.978)	1.814 (1.381)
Born Again Evangelical	−0.095 (1.404)	−0.214 (1.179)	-0.469 (0.411)
Political variables			
Party ID (more Republican)	−0.326 (0.408)		−3.419* (0.411)
Ideology (more conservative)	−0.968 (0.503)		−1.431* (0.591)
Feeling thermometers			
Barbara Bush	0.117* (0.035)	0.121* (0.028)	0.069 (0.036)
George Bush	−0.003 (0.031)	−0.039 (0.024)	
Bill Clinton	0.549* (0.031)	0.567* (0.023)	
Feminists	0.153* (0.030)	0.145* (0.024)	0.279* (0.034)
Constant	11.024* (4.448)	7.481* (3.188)	47.395 (4.730)
Adjusted R^2	0.519	0.518	0.312
N	755	987	756

Note: Parameter estimates are unstandardized regression coefficients with standard errors in parentheses. Data are from the 1992 ANES

$^*p < 0.05$

public opinion toward Hillary Clinton was not just less warm but also more polarized than views toward Barbara Bush. Among ANES respondents, 72 percent rated Barbara Bush positively (higher than 50), 17 percent were neutral in their rating, and 12 percent rated her negatively (below 50 degrees). In contrast, only 50 percent of respondents gave Hillary Clinton a rating above 50 degrees, 28 percent were neutral, and 21 rated her negatively. While Hillary Clinton provoked a much more polarized response from the public than Barbara Bush, with fewer respondents viewing Hillary Clinton favorably and more viewing her negatively than Barbara Bush, the fact that close to one-third of Americans viewed Hillary Clinton neutrally during the 1992 election is interesting. Over the next four years as first lady, Hillary Clinton not only became a household name but developed into an even more polarizing figure (Prysby and Scavo 2001).

Gender and Feminism

The election of 1992 is commonly referred to as the "Year of the Woman" due to a surge in female congressional candidates that set records at the time (Burrell 1994). Moreover, both of the candidate spouses spoke about their experiences as women and sought to appeal to women in their campaign appearances (Ifill 1992; Mughan and Burden 1995, 145). Barbara Bush's prime-time convention speech also leaned heavily on the traditionally feminine themes of motherhood and family (Vigil 2014). Given this and the reality that Barbara Bush and Hillary Clinton were two of the few women on the presidential campaign trail, there was reason to suspect women might respond particularly warmly to these two women.

There are also reasons to suspect those identifying as feminists may have felt a particularly strong sense of connection to Hillary Clinton in 1992. In the aftermath of confirmation hearings for Supreme Court Justice Clarence Thomas, where he was accused of sexual harassment by a former Equal Employment Opportunity Commission employee Anita Hill, many women's groups were outraged by her treatment by the all-male US Senate Judiciary Committee. The reaction to this incident sparked activism among feminist women who also rallied around the non-traditional role Hillary Clinton promised to play as first spouse. Additionally, previous research has also demonstrated that attitudes toward abortion were one of the key issues in influencing vote choice during the 1992 election and that attitudes toward reproductive rights were particularly salient for voters with feminist values (Abramowitz 1995). In the context of these social and political dynamics, Hillary Clinton held the potential to generate greater support both among women and individuals who embrace feminist values. To test the latter hypothesis, the multivariate models include an ANES feeling thermometer question gauging respondents' feelings toward feminists following the same measurement strategy used in other public opinion research on presidential candidate spouses (Elder and Frederick 2017).

Figure 3.3 shows that Barbara Bush generated strong support from both men and women but that women viewed her slightly more favorably than men, with ratings of 68 degrees and 65 degrees, respectively. Women also expressed more positive attitudes toward her as the relationship between sex and the dependent variable is statistically significant in all three of the multivariate models ($p < 0.05$). In the full model specification, holding all the other independent variables at their means, women rate Barbara Bush 5 degrees more favorably on the feeling thermometer scale than men. While George H. W. Bush did not fare as well among women as he did among men, in 1992, Barbara Bush was able to attract greater support from women. These results support the idea that women felt a special connection to Barbara Bush. Heightened support from women also helps explain Barbara Bush's very high favorable ratings.

Although Hillary Clinton challenged many of the traditional gender norms in her approach to the position of first lady, that image did not translate into major differences in her evaluations among men and women in the 1992 election. Women viewed her slightly more favorably on average than men, with mean feeling thermometer ratings of 57 and 54, respectively. The multivariate analyses, however, show that women's support for Hillary Clinton was statistically indistinguishable from men. In most of her future political career, Hillary Clinton would provoke much starker divisions along gender lines, but in 1992, it did not appear that the political forces that would drive this gap had fully taken shape yet. Hillary Clinton's untraditional approach to being a candidate spouse tapped into some of the fraught divisions among women, including the emotionally sensitive territory of working mothers. This may help explain why women were fairly divided in their response to her.

While Hillary Clinton was not any more warmly received among women than men, the regression models predicting warmth toward Hillary Clinton did produce some gendered relationships. In all three of the multivariate models (Table 3.3), feminist views were positively related to feelings toward her in 1992 ($p < 0.05$). Hillary Clinton's successful career in the legal profession and a willingness to speak on important policy questions sparked support from individuals with pro-feminist leanings and greater opposition from those individuals with anti-feminist views. In this way then, Hillary Clinton as a presidential candidate spouse can be viewed as providing symbolic representation to those with feminist sympathies. In contrast, Table 3.2 shows no discernable relationship between feminist attitudes and evaluations of Barbara Bush. This result confirms that her traditional approach as first lady did not tap into a pro-feminist consciousness in the same way Hillary Clinton did.

Age

The 1992 election represented a watershed for generational change in American politics, as Bill Clinton was the first Baby Boomer nominated as a presidential candidate of one of the two major parties (Maraniss 1995).

The Clintons campaigning on the theme of "two for the price of one" reflected a new idea, that the female spouses of major politicians would act as autonomous beings and have independent input on policy and decision-making. For older generations of Americans, this change may have signaled an unwanted disruption in the status quo of gender roles for the spouses of presidential candidates. Therefore it is reasonable to expect that these developments could translate into more positive evaluations among older individuals for Barbara Bush, and more positive evaluations for Hillary Clinton among younger people.

As Fig. 3.3 shows, Barbara Bush's support cut across age lines, with a feeling thermometer rating above 66 from all groups except 18–29-year-olds who rated her at 62 degrees. These numbers are consistent with older generations being very comfortable with Barbara Bush's style as first lady, while the youngest generation in 1992 was not quite as enthralled with her but still tended to view her quite warmly. Table 3.2, showing the multivariate regression models predicting support for Barbara Bush, reveals that in all three models, older, more highly educated, and wealthier Americans expressed more favorable views toward Barbara Bush ($p < 0.05$) than other groups. This result is consistent with the bivariate results, indicating older Americans were largely supportive of the traditional image Barbara Bush cultivated as first lady.

In contrast, there were few age differences in support for Hillary Clinton. Her highest level of support, perhaps surprisingly, was among individuals 65 years and older, who gave her an average feeling thermometer score of 57. Although she was challenging the conventional norms of what a model first lady should be, it did not seem to cost her disproportionate support among the generation with the most conservative cultural values. Part of this support could be attributed to members of the New Deal generation who gave more favorable evaluations because of their long-standing support for the Democratic Party. While one may have thought younger generations would be more open to the more modern and feminist image Hillary Clinton offered, this idea was not supported in the data. Age was not a significant predictor in the multivariate models predicting warmth toward Hillary Clinton.

Race

The racial divide is among the most enduring in American politics, and evaluations of presidential spouses are not exempt from this pattern

(Burrell et al. 2011). Although he distanced himself from major African American leaders like Reverend Jesse Jackson and campaigned as a more centrist Democrat, Bill Clinton still won overwhelming support from African American voters in the 1992 election. It is reasonable to expect that this support should have been transferable to Hillary Clinton. In contrast, although Barbara Bush largely shied away from policy pronouncements during her husband's administration, including civil rights, given her ties to the Republican Party she should have higher evaluations among White Americans than African Americans.

Figure 3.3 shows that the only demographic group rating Barbara Bush below 60 degrees was the African Americans group, where her support averaged 52 degrees on the feeling thermometer scale. Even that relatively low rating is testament to her popularity, as most Republicans do far worse in appealing for support among the African American community. Barbara Bush was also well received among Hispanics with a mean rating of 69. That said, the multivariate results (Table 3.2) suggest that once other potentially confounding factors are controlled, African Americans and Hispanics viewed her more negatively than Whites in all three models ($p < 0.05$). Although communities of color viewed Barbara Bush more warmly than they viewed most Republicans, Barbara Bush was not able to completely overcome the negative image most Republicans suffer from in the eyes of most African Americans and Hispanics. A bit of caution is warranted, however, when interpreting the result regarding Hispanics, since ANES included such a small sample of Hispanics in the 1992 survey.[2]

Besides liberals and Democrats, the only group with which Hillary Clinton fared better than Barbara Bush was the African Americans group that gave her an average rating of 64 compared to the 52 for Barbara Bush. In one of the multivariate model specifications predicting feelings toward Hillary Clinton, African Americans viewed her more positively at the conventional level of statistical significance ($p < 0.05$). As the most loyal Democratic constituency in the US population, these results are in line with expectations. However, Hillary Clinton's rating among African Americans did not reach the stratospheric level of support that Michelle Obama received from African Americans in the 2008 and 2012 presidential campaigns, as discussed in more detail in the following chapter. Hillary Clinton would eventually improve her standing among this crucial Democratic group of voters as her political career progressed, as the 89 percent support from African Americans she received in the 2016 presidential election reveals (Sabato 2017), but in 1992, as a non-incumbent spouse of a presidential candidate who espoused more conservative leaning policies than recent Democratic nominees, her rating among African Americans were not quite as stellar.

White Evangelicals

Another group of citizens resistant to changes in the gender norms represented by Hillary Clinton's ascendancy was White Evangelical Christians. This group was already moving toward a long-term allegiance with the Republican Party during the Ronald Reagan Presidency based on that party's embrace of more conservative social policies (Wilcox and Robinson 2011). The contrast between the traditional Barbara Bush and the more feminist Hillary Clinton may have driven White Evangelicals even closer to the Republican Party during the 1992 campaign. At the very least, given the contrast in their views of the appropriate role of a first lady, one would expect Barbara Bush's ratings among this group would be noticeably higher than Hillary Clinton's ratings.

Figure 3.3 shows that Barbara Bush did in fact achieve a high rating among White Evangelicals at 72 degrees, confirming our expectations that not only had this group become a key base of support for national Republicans but also was quite receptive to a first lady who conformed to traditional profile in this position. Multivariate analysis consistently shows that White Evangelicals viewed Barbara Bush more favorably, but this relationship was only statistically significant in one of the three model specifications. Not surprisingly, Hillary Clinton's average rating among White Evangelicals was 20 points lower than it was for Barbara Bush at 52 points. However, given her advocacy of many pro-feminist positions and her embrace of a non-traditional profile for the position of first lady, the fact that she had a slightly positive rating among this group is a bit surprising. Perhaps being married to a White Evangelical Southerner allowed her to mitigate some of her potential unpopularity among this demographic.

Partisanship and Ideology

Since the early days of conducting scientific public opinion polls survey, researchers have observed the power of partisanship to filter the perceptions of individual citizens about various aspects of American politics (Campbell et al. 1960). Even if citizens know very little about a political issue or candidate, there is common tendency to rely on one's long-standing partisan attachments to help them make a judgment about how to evaluate them absent complete information. This pattern of partisanship has been observed in multiple studies of attitudes toward the spouses of presidential candidates (Burrell et al. 2011; Elder and Frederick 2017; Sulfaro 2007). The 1992 election should be no exception to this trend. As Chap. 2 showed (Fig. 2.4), Democrats evaluated Hillary Clinton more favorably, while Republicans evaluated Barbara Bush more favorably. Nevertheless, given Barbara Bush's overwhelming popularity, it makes sense to predict that opinions toward her should be less polarized by partisanship than Hillary Clinton. However, it should be noted that while Hillary Clinton was a lightning rod for criticism among Republicans in 1992, as discussed earlier in this chapter, the level of criticism did not reach the heights that it did when she served as head of the health care taskforce during Bill Clinton's presidency in 1993 and 1994 (Burrell 2001).

Ideology has also been shown to shape perceptions of presidential candidate spouses (Elder and Frederick 2017). Although partisanship and ideology have become more strongly correlated in recent years (Abramowitz 2010; Campbell 2016), Americans are not sorted perfectly along partisan and ideological lines (Ellis and Stimson 2012). Considering Hillary Clinton's willingness to speak out on various policy issues during the 1992 campaign, conservatives should have been expected to react more negatively to her than liberals. One caveat is in order that might diminish ideological evaluations of Hillary Clinton. In 1992, Bill Clinton ran as a so-called New Democrat echoing more conservative themes on crime, welfare, and the economy than previous Democratic presidential candidates (Hale 1995), a campaign theme Hillary Clinton also openly championed. Perhaps this attempt to embrace centrism would help her garner more support among moderates and conservatives than the spouse of a more conventional liberal nominee. Barbara Bush shied away from policy involvement in the Bush administration, which may have helped diminish the extent of ideological reactions to her persona. However, given her association with President Bush, liberals should view her in a more negative light than moderates or conservatives.

Figure 3.3 shows that Barbara Bush's highest average rating is among Republicans at 76, but she also gets positive ratings from Independents and Democrats at 67 and 62, respectively. She is also viewed quite favorably across the ideological spectrum, with ratings above 60 from conservatives, moderates, and liberals. From the perspective of today's polarized climate, it is impressive to see a national political figure transcend partisan and ideological lines the way Barbara Bush did in 1992.

Examining these political variables in the multivariate models reveals that conservatives and Republicans viewed Barbara Bush more positively but only in the model excluding the evaluations of the presidential candidates. It is not surprising that these relationships would not hold up considering partisanship and ideology are so strongly correlated with the views of the candidates. Controlling for the other variables in the model, strong Republicans viewed Barbara Bush 18 degrees more favorably than strong Democrats, and conservatives viewed her 12 degrees more favorably than liberals. Although her popularity was overwhelming across the political spectrum, Barbara Bush was still viewed through a partisan or ideological prism to a degree.

A partisan gap also existed in support for Hillary Clinton, with the Democrats average rating recorded at 63, Independents at 53, and Republicans at 46 degrees. The partisan gap between Democrats and Republicans of 17 degrees was only slightly higher than the gap for Barbara Bush of 14. There was also an ideological divide in evaluations of Hillary Clinton, but her average rating was in positive territory among liberals, moderates, and conservatives. Liberals' average rating of 63 and conservatives' average rating of 51 reflected some degree of ideological polarization but not nearly the same level of division that would be present during the Health Care debate of President Bill Clinton's first two years in office (Burrell 2001).

The results in Table 3.3 show that coefficients for partisanship and ideology were in the expected directions. In the model excluding perceptions of the presidential candidates, stronger identification with the Republican Party and more conservative views were negatively related to feelings toward Hillary Clinton. The magnitude of effects was comparable to Barbara Bush's ratings, with partisanship having a slightly stronger impact and ideology, somewhat surprisingly, slightly less of an impact than it did for Barbara Bush.

These findings are interesting for several reasons. One is that while Barbara Bush was less polarizing than Hillary Clinton, the difference was not dramatic. Thus, while Hillary Clinton was viewed in a partisan light in 1992, she was not yet as polarizing as she would be after four years in the national spotlight as first lady and at later points of her independent political career. As the previous chapter shows, views toward Hillary Clinton in 1992 were not only less polarized than views of Hillary Clinton in 1996, but also less polarized than views of Teresa Heinz Kerry in 2004, as well as all candidate spouses from 2008 to the present. While partisanship and ideology significantly shaped attitudes of both candidate spouses in 1992, views were much less dictated by partisanship than they would become two decades later.

The degree to which presidential candidate spouses were able to rise above partisan and ideological polarizations in 1992 certainly allowed Barbara Bush more room to develop markedly high approval ratings. Additionally, these results show that partisan polarization alone cannot account for the relative unpopularity of Hillary Clinton compared to Barbara Bush. Hillary Clinton was viewed less warmly by her own party than Barbara Bush was viewed by her party. This finding suggests Hillary Clinton's untraditional performance as a candidate spouse led to lower approval ratings across the political spectrum, not just from Republicans and/or conservatives.

Presidential Candidate Perceptions

Besides partisanship and ideology, one of the strongest predictors of individual-level support for the spouses is support for the presidential candidates themselves (Elder and Frederick 2017). This relationship makes sense since the public knows most spouses only through their connection to the candidates themselves. Chapter 2 shows that both Barbara Bush and Hillary Clinton had higher favorable ratings during the 1992 campaign than their husbands. The gulf between Barbara Bush and her husband was particularly large, with Barbara Bush having the highest net favorable ratings on record, while her husband George W. Bush is one of four candidates in the timeline with net negative favorable ratings (the other three were Michael Dukakis in 1988, Hillary Clinton in 2016, and Donald Trump in 2016). These bivariate comparisons showcase both the relative popularity of spouses compared to the candidates, and the autonomy of public perceptions toward them.

The multivariate models incorporate views of both presidential candidates as predictors of support for the spouses. Including evaluations of the opposition candidate in the model helps to capture the feelings of individuals who may base their evaluation of the spouse as a function of their feelings toward opposing presidential candidate as a filter. For instance, some voters' evaluations of Hillary Clinton could have been shaped in part from how they viewed President Bush.

The multivariate model specifications also include the feeling thermometer ratings of the opposing candidate spouse as independent variables. Original survey data discussed in Chap. 2 show that some Americans believe that candidate spouses should be viewed with more sympathy than other individuals campaigning on behalf of the president. Thus, there may be some people predisposed to like all candidate spouses regardless of party. Indeed, previous research has also shown that evaluations of the opposing candidate spouses are positively related to one another (Elder and Frederick 2017).

The results for the feeling thermometer variables are in the hypothesized direction. Attitudes toward George Bush were positively related to evaluations of Barbara Bush ($p < 0.05$). Controlling for the other independent variables in the models, every one degree increase in George Bush's feeling thermometer rating is associated with a 0.45 degree increase in Barbara Bush's feeling thermometer rating. This relationship is the strongest among the affective predictors of support for Barbara Bush, yet at the same time it is important to point out that views of George H. W. Bush were not completely determinative in shaping views of Barbara Bush. Also, as expected, feelings toward Bill Clinton are negatively related to support for Barbara Bush, but the magnitude of the relationship is noticeably weaker. All else equal, a one degree increase in support for Bill Clinton corresponds to a 0.118 decrease in support for Barbara Bush. Having a favorable view of Bill Clinton only marginally decreases support for Barbara Bush.

As with Barbara Bush, the strongest predictor of support for Hillary Clinton in 1992 are views of Bill Clinton. Controlling for the other variables in the models, an increase of one degree of support for Bill Clinton led to a 0.55 degree in support for Hillary Clinton ($p < 0.05$). Those who liked Bill Clinton tended to like Hillary Clinton. Unlike with Barbara Bush, attitudes toward the opposing presidential candidate George H. W. Bush were not significantly related to views toward Hillary Clinton.

Consistent with survey research presented in Chap. 2 that show that some Americans feel that candidate spouses should be viewed with greater sympathy than other campaign surrogates, feelings toward the 1992 spouses were positively related to one another. In two of three model specifications, views of Barbara Bush were positively related to views of Hillary Clinton and vice versa. These results are consistent with the idea that a certain segment of the population is warmly disposed toward presidential candidate spouses in general regardless of party, and conversely, that some voters negatively view the spouses regardless of party.

Discussion and Conclusion

The 1992 election featured two very distinct candidate spouses representing vastly different conceptions of the presidential wife and highlighting the changing role of women in society. Barbara Bush embodied the traditional role of first lady, and she faced off against Hillary Clinton who challenged the traditional boundaries of this role (Shoop 2010).

Barbara Bush remains to this day the most popular presidential candidate spouse in modern polling history. Her background and approach to the role were highly traditional, but she layered on to this traditional approach a decidedly active role as surrogate for her husband, thereby laying the groundwork for new traditionalism. By making the case for her husband in a highly visible way throughout the 1992 campaign while conforming to traditional expectations, she was able to garner impressive and unparalleled support from the American public, while leading very few people to develop unfavorable views of her. Her decision to embrace and highlight the traditional role of candidate spouse resulted in very few pollster inquiries as well as very high levels of support across the political spectrum, from both Republicans and Democrats, liberals and conservatives. Throughout her four years as first lady, Barbara Bush was able to draw on the institutional perquisites of the office to shape her image and demonstrate in a concrete way that she comported to the public's expectations about how presidential spouses should behave, and the public grew to like her even more.

Through the analyses employing ANES data, this chapter was able to examine which groups in particular felt warmly toward Barbara Bush, and the answer is almost everybody. As an incumbent first lady who conformed to traditional public conceptions of how spouses should behave in that position, she was particularly beloved among older, conservative, and evangelical Americans, but by operating within the traditional role she was also able to cultivate a broad base of support among a wide range of Americans that was quite impressive.

Barbara Bush was particularly beloved among women, which is quite unusual for a Republican political figure, as it reverses the contours of the typical gender gap characterizing partisanship and political evaluations begun in the 1980s. This is consistent with the idea that women felt a particular connection to Barbara Bush. In the male-dominated world of presidential politics, Barbara Bush was speaking about women's issues and appealing to women, and women in turn gave her distinctively warm evaluations. Thus, a key to understanding Barbara Bush as the most popular candidate spouse and first lady is to understand the symbolic role she played in speaking for and connecting with women.

In dramatic contrast to Barbara Bush, Hillary Clinton broke the boundaries of a presidential candidate's spouse (Shoop 2010), representing a facet of contemporary feminism and the second wave of the women's movement. "Hillary Clinton had added a substantive focus to the campaign, however, controversial, that citizens were able to reflect upon for the first time" (Burrell 2001, 32). Hillary Clinton's role and performance in the 1992 election campaign presented in stark relief the challenge of contemporary feminism to the traditional idea of a first lady (Troy 2006).

The result in terms of public opinion was a more divided public response, as reflected in 1992 ANES thermometer scores and average favorable and unfavorable ratings from national polls taken during the presidential campaign. Hillary Clinton was viewed significantly less favorably than Barbara Bush, with an adjusted favorable average of 55 percent compared to Barbara Bush's 88 percent. That said, it is important to note that, on average, during the 1992 campaign, more people expressed favorable views of Hillary Clinton than unfavorable views—and she was not as polarizing a figure as she would become across the next four years as first lady (Burrell 2001; Prysby and Scavo 2001). While those favorably disposed toward feminism viewed Hillary Clinton warmly, in keeping with the theory of symbolic representation, Hillary Clinton's favorable ratings suffered in comparison to Barbara Bush among almost every group. Not just Republicans but Democrats too reacted to her in a less than favorable way than they did to Barbara Bush, reflecting the discomfort many Americans have with a more egalitarian, less traditional approach to the role of candidate spouse.

After becoming first lady, Hillary Clinton took a gamble in the first years of the Clinton administration when she headed the health care reform taskforce. Early opinion research showed a positive reaction among the public for her taking on this task, but as the Clintons faltered in their attempt and became mired in the Whitewater scandal, she took a public relations beating and retreated from being a public domestic policy adviser (Burrell 2001). Thus, expectations for a spouse who was both active and traditional, a combination we refer to as new traditionalism, were heightened and reinforced.

The markedly different ways the public responded to Barbara Bush and Hillary Clinton across the 1992 campaign and as first ladies profoundly altered the campaign world for future presidential candidate spouses. The negative press coverage and opposition scrutiny Hillary Clinton received as a candidate spouse, and even more as first lady (Burrell 2001), appears to have lain a shadow over the performance of subsequent would-be first lady candidates, even for those who would be considered professional and policy-oriented women. Candidate spouses including Laura Bush, Tipper Gore, as well as Michelle Obama and Ann Romney, who are the focus of the next chapter, were careful to thread the needle of new traditionalism as candidate spouses. For the most part, these spouses widely engaged in their spouse's campaign but held back from expressing an independent voice or any desire to influence politics or policy on the campaign trail.

Notes

1. Eleanor Roosevelt, for example, did not campaign on behalf of her husband. Yet, President Lyndon Johnson's wife was strategically sent to campaign in the south during the 1964 campaign since she had broader appeal in that region than her husband (Tien et al. 1999, 160 and 150).
2. The number of Hispanics in the 1992 ANES was 11 respondents, which was less than one percent of the entire sample.

Bibliography

Abramowitz, Alan I. 1995. It's Abortion, Stupid: Policy Voting in the 1992 Presidential Election. *Journal of Politics* 57 (1): 176–186.

———. 2010. *The Disappearing Center: Engaged Citizens, Polarization, and American Democracy*. New Haven, CT: Yale University Press.

Burrell, Barbara. 1994. *A Woman's Place Is in the House: Campaigning for Congress in the Feminist Era*. Ann Arbor, MI: University of Michigan Press.

———. 2001. *Public Opinion, the First Ladyship, and Hillary Rodham Clinton*. New York: Routledge.

Burrell, Barbara, Laurel Elder, and Brian Frederick. 2011. From Hillary to Michelle: Public Opinion and the Spouses of Presidential Candidates. *Presidential Studies Quarterly* 41 (1): 156–176.

Campbell, James E. 2016. *Polarized: Making Sense of a Divided America*. Princeton, NJ: Princeton University Press.

Campbell, Angus, Phillip E. Converse, Warren E. Miller, and Donald E. Stokes. 1960. *The American Voter*. Chicago, IL: University of Chicago Press.

Caroli, Betty Boyd. 2010. *First Ladies: From Martha Washington to Michelle Obama*. Oxford: Oxford University.

Cooper, Matthew. 1992. The Hillary Factor. *U.S. News & World Report*, April 27, 32–37.

Elder, Laurel, and Brian Frederick. 2017. Perceptions of Candidate Spouses in the 2012 Presidential Election: The Role of Gender, Race, Religion, and Partisanship. *Politics, Groups, and Identities*. https://doi.org/10.1080/21565503.2017.1338969

Ellis, Christopher, and James Stimson. 2012. *Ideology in America*. Cambridge: Cambridge University Press.

Friedman, Jaclyn. 2012. First Ladies in Waiting. *The American Prospect*, October 24. http://prospect.org/article/first-ladies-waiting

Hale, Jon F. 1995. The Making of the New Democrats. *Political Science Quarterly* 119 (2): 207–232.

Ifill, Gwen. 1992. The 1992 Campaign: Democrats; Trapped in a Spotlight, Hillary Clinton Uses It. *The New York Times*, February 3.

Keen, Judy. 1992. In Bush's Corner, a First Lady Who Is a Fighter. *USA Today*, October 9.

Maraniss, David. 1995. *First in His Class: The Biography of Bill Clinton*. New York: Simon and Schuster.

Monastra, Pamela. 1992. A Vote for 'MOM' Barbara Bush Wows Crowd on Campaign Stop. *Atlanta Journal and Constitution*, October 2.

Morrison, Patt. 1992. Time for a Feminist as First Lady? *Los Angeles Times*, July 14.

Mughan, Anthony, and Barry C. Burden. 1995. The Candidates' Wives. In *Democracy's Feast: Elections in America*, ed. Herbert F. Weisberg. Chatham, NJ: Chatham House.

Prysby, Charles, and Carmine Scavo. 2001. Who Hates Hillary? Public Opinion Toward the First Lady, 1992–1996. *Politics & Policy* 29 (3): 521–542.

Quindlen, Anna. 1992. Public and Private; the Two Faces of Eve. *New York Times*, July 15.

Radcliffe, Donnie. 1992. First Lady Gets the Third Degree; On the Stump, Barbara Warms Them Up. But George Burns Them Up. *Washington Post*, February 6.

Rosenthal, Harry. 1992. Bush, Launching Campaign, Takes a Ride on First Lady's Popularity. *Associated Press*, February 12.

Sabato, Larry J. 2017. The Election That Broke All or At Least Most of the Rules. In *Trumped the Election that Broke All of the Rules*, ed. Larry J. Sabato, Kyle Kondik, and Geoffrey Skelly, 1–29. Lanham, MD: Rowman and Littlefield.

Sheehy, Gail. 1992. What Hillary Wants. *Vanity Fair*, May.

Shoop, Tiffany J. 2010. From Professionals to Potential First Ladies: How Newspapers Told the Stories of Cindy McCain and Michelle Obama. *Sex Roles* 63: 807–819.

Stanley, Alessandra. 1992. The 1992 Campaign: Barbara Bush; First Lady on Abortion, "Not a Platform Issue". *New York Times*, August 14.

Sulfaro, Valerie. 2007. Affective Evaluations of First Ladies: A Comparison of Hillary Clinton and Laura Bush. *Presidential Studies Quarterly* 37: 486–514.

Tien, Charles, Regan Checchio, and Arthur H. Miller. 1999. The Impact of First Wives on Presidential Campaigns and Elections. In *Women in Politics: Outsiders or Insiders?* ed. Lois Duke Whitaker, 149–168. Upper Saddle River, NJ: Prentice Hall.

Troy, Gil. 2006. *Hillary Clinton: Polarizing First Lady*. Lawrence, KS: Kansas University Press.

U.S. News and World Report. 1992. PSRA/U.S. News & World Report Poll, Apr, 1992 [survey question]. USPSRA.NW0492.R07. Princeton Survey Research Associates [producer]. Cornell University, Ithaca, NY: Roper Center for Public Opinion Research, iPOLL [distributor]. Accessed October 11, 2017.

Vigil, Tammy R. 2014. Feminine Views in the Feminine Style: Convention Speeches by Presidential Nominees' Spouses. *Southern Communication Journal* 79: 327–346.

Wilcox, Cyde, and Carin Robinson. 2011. *Onward Christian Soldier: The Religious Right in American Politics*. 4th ed. Boulder, CO: Westview Press.

CHAPTER 4

Historic Firsts: Public Opinion Toward Michelle Obama and Ann Romney in the 2012 Presidential Election

In the summer of the 2012, Michelle Obama and Ann Romney gave barrier-breaking speeches at the Democratic and Republican National Conventions. On September 4, 2012, Michelle Obama earned the distinction of being the first African American woman to address a national political convention as first lady of the United States. One week earlier, Ann Romney addressed the Republican National Convention, becoming the first Mormon woman to speak as the spouse of a presidential candidate nominated by major political party in the United States. Despite their historical significance, neither Michelle Obama nor Ann Romney decided to highlight the groundbreaking aspects of their biographies. Instead, they used their speeches to illuminate the personal character of their husbands, urging the voters to entrust them with the presidency. Both women also emphasized their credentials as mothers and made the case that their husbands would be good presidents because they are good family men (Duerst-Lahti 2014; Elder and Greene 2016; Vigil 2014). News stories noted that both Ann Romney and Michelle Obama were more popular than their husbands (e.g. Craighill and Eastabrooks 2012). And both were labeled by the news media as their husbands' "secret weapon" (Cottle 2012).

This chapter analyzes public perceptions of the 2012 presidential candidate spouses, Michelle Obama and Ann Romney, paying particular attention to the role of gender, race, and religion, as well as partisanship and candidate perceptions in shaping attitudes. It draws on 2012 ANES data and aggregate survey results from the Roper Center for

L. Elder et al., *American Presidential Candidate Spouses*,
https://doi.org/10.1007/978-3-319-73879-6_4

Public Opinion Research to further our understanding of what factors contributed to their popularity in the eyes of the American public. The data lend further support to the theoretical frameworks outlined in previous chapters.

Although Michelle Obama and Ann Romney had contrasting personalities and backgrounds, they adopted similar approaches to the role of presidential candidate spouse. Both women embodied the expectations of new traditionalism—serving as highly visible campaign surrogates for their husbands while embracing a traditionally gendered role that avoided mention of any major policy influence—and both were rewarded with a warm embrace from the public. Indeed, by embodying the expectations of new traditionalism, Michelle Obama benefited from a large increase in favorable ratings through incumbency advantage to become one of the most popular first ladies of the modern era. The data also show that Michelle Obama in particular offered symbolic inspiration for historically underrepresented groups. Finally, while both Michelle Obama and Ann Romney generated polarized reactions along partisan and ideological lines, their embrace of new traditionalism helped them to rise above the partisan fray to some degree and establish identities as autonomous political entities even as attitudes toward Mitt Romney and Barack Obama shaped feelings toward them.

New Traditionalism and Symbolic Firsts

The 1992 presidential campaign marked a turning point in terms of the role of presidential spouses. Although strikingly different in their approaches to the role of presidential spouse, both Barbara Bush and Hillary Clinton were prominent campaign surrogates, contributing to the now common political expectation that the spouses of presidential candidates will be vigorous advocates on behalf of their spouses' campaigns for the White House. The 2012 presidential election strongly reinforced this expectation as Michelle Obama and Ann Romney used their public appearances to advocate on behalf of their spouses President Barack Obama and former Massachusetts Governor Mitt Romney, respectively. As one journalist observed in reference to the spouses of the 2012 major party nominees for president, "Both fought fiercely for their husbands, and both proved gifted surrogates" (Cottle 2012).

While the news media generally agreed that both Michelle Obama and Ann Romney were gifted campaigners and assets to their husbands' efforts to win election, the media also highlighted their contrasting personal histories—Michelle Obama used her law degree in several high-powered jobs prior to becoming a candidate spouse, while Ann Romney focused her work in the private sphere, raising five children and volunteering in her community (e.g. Davidson 2012; Groer 2012; Von Drehle 2012). This difference received considerable publicity when a Democratic consultant Hilary Rosen stated in a TV interview that Ann Romney had "never worked a day in her life" (Kucinich and Moore 2012). Their personalities and stylistic sensibilities were also quite different. Michelle Obama became a bit of a fashion icon for many women, while Ann Romney's style did not garner the same attention. As a *Newsweek* story stated, "It is rare that a presidential race brings us two spouses that embody such contrasting versions of first ladydom—really of American culture more broadly. Michelle Obama: modern, striving, edgy, ironic. Ann Romney: traditional, genteel, vulnerable, soothing, earnest" (Cottle 2012).

Despite the differences in their backgrounds and stylistic choices, both Michelle Obama and Ann Romney embraced traditional themes and roles in their campaign appearances (Vigil 2014). Although she had a law degree and a high-powered career, in 2007, Michelle Obama put her career aside to devote herself to her husband's political ambitions and to raising their daughters. A focus on being "mom-in-chief" continued through her first four years as first lady and throughout the 2012 campaign (Hayden 2017; Guerrero 2011; Kahl 2009; Vigil 2014). Ann Romney also drew the nation's attention to her work as a wife and mother in her campaign appearances (Vigil 2014).

Even with their active campaign schedules, neither Ann Romney nor Michelle Obama used their platforms to emphasize their own accomplishments outside of their roles as mothers or discuss plans for influencing administrative decisions or policy development, as Hillary Clinton had done two decades earlier. In other words, despite the differences in their personalities and styles, Michelle Obama and Ann Romney both conformed to, rather than challenged, gendered conceptions of the role played by presidential candidate spouses. Indeed, by serving as highly visible campaign surrogates across the 2012 election season while embracing a traditional role that avoided mention of any major policy influence, Michelle Obama and Ann Romney not only embodied but reinforced modern expectations for candidate spouses, which this study labels new traditionalism.

While embracing new traditionalism in terms of their actions and comportment as candidate spouses, Michelle Obama and Ann Romney were, at the same time, groundbreaking in important ways. Michelle Obama made history as the first African American woman to serve as first lady of the United States (Caroli 2010; Griffin 2011; Parks and Roberson 2009). Meanwhile, Ann and Mitt Romney were the first Mormon major party couple running for president. Thus, the presence of these two women on the campaign trail brought issues of race and religion into the public's view in a prominent way that contrasted noticeably from spouses of the past. They had the potential to stimulate the feelings of connection to presidential politics from Mormons and African Americans in ways no presidential candidate spouses had ever done before. They also could spark greater support among individuals who viewed those groups favorably and provoke hostile reactions among those who viewed them more negatively (Elder and Frederick 2017; Knuckey and Kim 2016). Thus, the 2012 election provides an excellent opportunity to explore further the theoretical framework of symbolic representation developed in prior chapters.

Attitudes Toward Michelle Obama and Ann Romney over the 2012 Campaign Season

In order to get a better sense of their overall standing in the minds of the American public, Figs. 4.1 and 4.2 plot the favorability of the presidential candidate spouses across the 2012 campaign, from January 2012 through Election Day. As an incumbent, first lady Michelle Obama was consider-

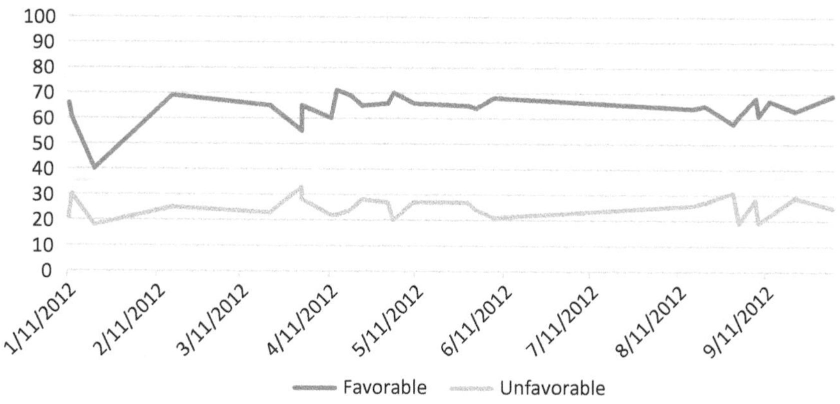

Fig. 4.1 Michelle Obama's favorable/unfavorable ratings over 2012 campaign

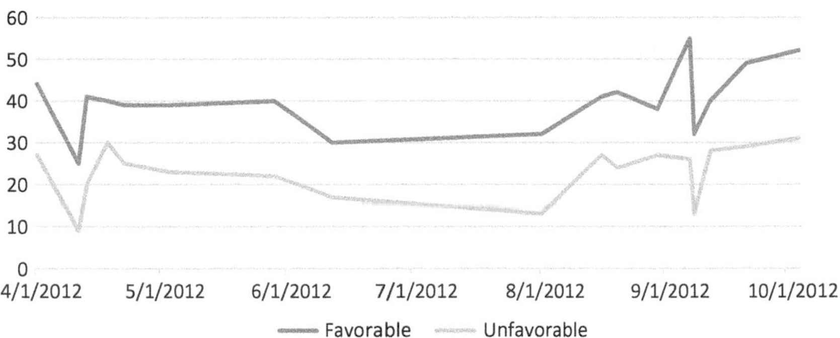

Fig. 4.2 Ann Romney's favorable/unfavorable ratings over 2012 campaign

ably more well-known than Ann Romney over the course of the campaign. This name recognition led to greater stability in the trend line of her favorability ratings.

In keeping with spouses who embody new traditionalism, Michelle Obama was quite popular, with a 65 percent average favorable rating and a 72 percent average adjusted favorable rating (see Figs. 2.2. and 2.3 in Chap. 2). These ratings mark her as the third most popular candidate spouse over the past 30 years after Barbara Bush and Laura Bush. As Fig. 4.1 shows, in only two of the 26 polls asking whether individuals had a favorable view of Michelle Obama over the course of the 2012 campaign did her rating drop below 60 percent. One of these deviations was a *CBS/New York Times* poll on January 20, which seems like an outlier in the series. Overall, there is very little movement in public perceptions of Michelle Obama in reaction to campaign events, as her ratings hovered between the mid-60s and low 70s. Michelle Obama was a popular first lady, and the 2012 election did little to dent that standing in the minds of most Americans. Conversely, the campaign did little to boost her already high ratings. Michelle Obama's ability to maintain such high favorable ratings throughout the hard-fought 2012 campaign is all the more impressive given the increased ideological and partisan polarization of American politics (Abramowitz 2011; Campbell 2016) and her status as the first African American first lady during a time of considerable racial acrimony (Abramowitz 2017; Czaja et al. 2015; Kinder and Dale-Riddle 2012; Tesler 2016; Tesler and Sears 2010).

As Fig. 4.2 shows, Ann Romney's ratings evinced much greater variation during the 2012 campaign. This pattern makes sense since she was relatively new to the national political scene, and it took some time before many Americans were willing to register an opinion of her. Until her speech at the Republican National Convention in August, over 30 percent of Americans did not express an opinion toward Ann Romney in all but one poll. However, once she did have the spotlight of the convention speech, her positive and negative ratings started to climb. In the final survey of the campaign asking a question about her, conducted by *ABC* and *The Washington Post* in early October, only 17 percent of Americans did not rate her. By this time, 52 percent of Americans rated her favorably and 32 percent unfavorably. As shown in Chap. 2, Ann Romney's adjusted favorable average, which takes into account those who could not rate her, was 64 as compared to Michelle Obama's 72 (Fig. 2.3). It is important to emphasize that Ann Romney made a positive impression on most Americans; she simply did not generate the same level of support Michelle Obama received from the public.

The incumbency advantage of serving as sitting first lady can explain much of the disparity in their favorability ratings. As Chap. 2 documents, Michelle Obama averaged a 44 percent favorability rating in 2008, which was only about four points higher than Ann Romney's 40 percent average favorability rating in 2012. And, in fact, Michelle Obama's adjusted favorability average in 2008 was 64, identical to Ann Romney's adjusted favorability average in 2012. Figure 4.3 displays the average favorability rating and adjusted favorability rating for incumbent and non-incumbent presidential candidate spouses in the period 1988–2016. This figure further illustrates that the ratings of Michelle Obama in 2008 and of Ann Romney in 2012 were close to the averages of non-incumbent spouses over the course of this study.

Like Barbara Bush and Laura Bush before her, Michelle Obama capitalized on the platform of being first lady and became even more warmly received by the public over her first four years as a presidential spouse (see Fig. 2.4 in Chap. 2). During her first four years as first lady, Michelle Obama focused on broadly popular issues—including children's health and supporting military families—consistent with the gendered norms of the position, and unlike Hillary Clinton, she did not play a high-profile policy role in her husband's administration. Michelle Obama also played an active role on the campaign trail as a surrogate for her husband, serving as an important validator of President Barack Obama's personal character

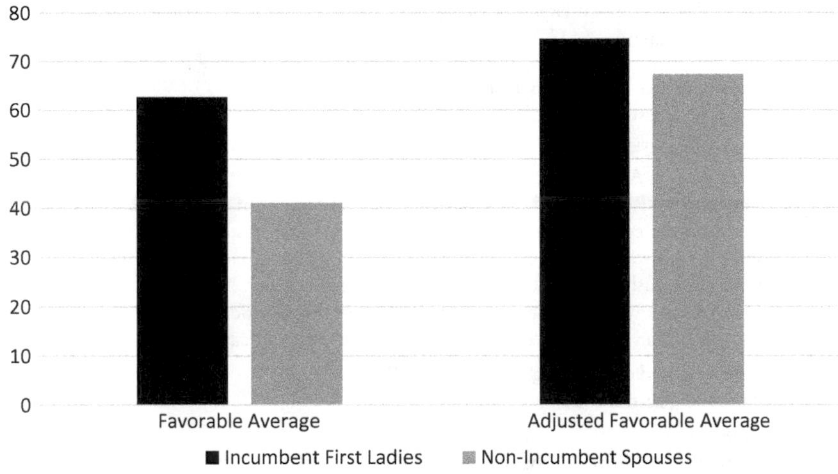

Fig. 4.3 Average favorable and adjusted favorable ratings for incumbent first ladies and non-incumbent presidential candidate spouses 1988–2016

in the minds of the American public. As a result, from 2008 to 2012, Michelle Obama was rewarded with a 21 percentage point increase in her favorable average and an 8 percentage point increase in her adjusted favorable average. Thus, Ann Romney was less popular than Michelle Obama in large part because she was a non-incumbent presidential candidate spouse, and not because of her personal profile or anything she did on the campaign trail. Both of the 2012 candidate spouses carefully conformed to the expectations of new traditionalism, and both were favorably received by the American public.

Pollster Inquiries

A close examination of pollster inquiries about the candidate spouses during the 2012 campaign, presented in Table 4.1, also illustrates the ways Michelle Obama and Ann Romney conformed to the public's expectations for this role. Over the 2012 campaign, 29 survey items inquired about Michelle Obama and 21 inquired about Ann Romney. Unlike 1992 (and 2016, which is discussed in the next chapter), the media polls during the 2012 campaign focused almost exclusively on whether respondents viewed the candidate spouses favorably, reflecting the non-controversial nature of

Table 4.1 Pollster inquiries about presidential candidate spouses during the 2012 campaign season

Poll questions asked about Ann Romney, 21
Favorability type questions (19)

Tailored questions (2)

- Did you watch Ann Romney's convention speech?
- Recently, Mitt Romney said his wife Ann tells him American women are particularly focused on the economy and jobs. A female Democratic strategist said Ann Romney, who was a stay-at-home mother of five children, had no credibility advising her husband on the economic issues facing women because, quote, "Ann Romney hasn't worked a day in her life." Do you think criticizing his wife is fair because Romney mentioned she advises him, or is this a cheap shot?

Poll questions asked about Michelle Obama, 29
Favorability type questions (28)

Tailored question (1)

- Did you watch Michelle Obama's convention speech?

Source: Polls archived at the Roper Center for Public Opinion Research

Ann Romney's and Michelle Obama's performances as presidential candidate spouses. All but three of the 50 total survey questions were the standard favorable/unfavorable queries. Of those three questions, there was one apiece asking respondents if they had seen their respective convention speeches. The only other tailored question asked about what people thought of comments made by Democratic Party strategist Hilary Rosen who argued on a CNN broadcast that Ann Romney lacked credibility speaking on women's and economic issues because "she hadn't worked a day in her life." This incident was a brief media controversy that disappeared rather quickly from public attention.

Overall, Ann Romney and Michelle Obama embodied modern expectations for presidential candidate spouses and avoided major controversies on the campaign trail. Neither Michelle Obama nor Ann Romney challenged gender norms or sought to play a major policy role in their spouse's administration the way Hillary Clinton did in 1992. The media responded by not including tailored survey items about them in major national polls as they did about Hillary Clinton in 1992. Unlike in 1992, there were no poll questions asking whether Michelle Obama or Ann Romney was too pushy, had too much influence, spent enough time with their families, or were too ambitious.

The major ways the 2012 candidate spouses did challenge the traditional status of first lady, through race in the case of Michelle Obama and religion in the case of Ann Romney, did not seem to interest the media outlets who conducted the polls. Each candidate spouse broke a historic barrier in their own right, but those accomplishments were not significant enough to generate media inquiries of the public about it during the 2012 campaign. This development was not simply a reaction to the novelty of Michelle Obama serving as the first African American first lady for four years, it mirrored the absence of media poll questions about the subject in 2008 (see Table 2.2 in Chap. 2). However, as shown in the analysis of the ANES public opinion data later on in this chapter, even if the media did not ask about these historic firsts, there were segments of the population who were acutely aware of their groundbreaking statuses as presidential spouses, and their support in public opinion polls reflected it.

Individual-Level Analysis

Michelle Obama and Ann Romney embodied modern expectations for candidate spouses in terms of their actions on the campaign trail, yet at the same time they challenged the traditional image of first ladies through their race and religion. This section of the chapter delves deeper into public perceptions of the 2012 candidate spouses by examining the individual-level factors that influence support for them. Fortunately, as was the case in 1992, the ANES included the feeling thermometer survey questions for both of the presidential candidate spouses in the 2012 survey. The 2012 feeling thermometer scores reinforce the favorability results discussed earlier in the chapter, indicating that Michelle Obama was viewed more favorably than Ann Romney. Michelle Obama had a mean rating of 65, while Ann Romney registered a 52. This gap in popularity is not driven by a significant variance in response frequency, as 91 percent of respondents could rate Michelle Obama compared to 89 from Ann Romney. Scrutinizing the dispersion of feeling thermometer responses supplies additional context to the top line percentages. For Ann Romney, 27 percent of respondents rated here negatively (lower than 50 degrees), 40 percent evaluated her favorably, and 33 percent of respondents gave her a neutral rating of 50 degrees on the feeling thermometer scale. The numbers for Michelle Obama show a similar 27 percent of respondents rating her negatively, while 12.5 percent gave her a neutral rating of 50 degrees. However, 60.5 percent gave her a positive rating (higher than 50 degrees), further suggesting Michelle Obama's greater name recognition translated into higher favorability scores.

The wealth of questions asked on the 2012 ANES provides the opportunity to examine which groups responded particularly warmly to Michelle Obama and Ann Romney, and to explore the extent to which Michelle Obama's and Ann Romney's embrace of new traditionalism allowed them to rise above partisan polarization and craft images independent of those of their husbands. By employing ANES data, this chapter is also able to explore whether the candidate spouses acted as symbolic representatives by looking at the degree to which groups represented descriptively by these two women viewed them favorably.

The chapter first presents bivariate analyses of the mean level of support among various demographic groups followed by multivariate regression analyses to assess which relationships hold up after appropriate statistical controls. Following the same practice established in Chap. 3, the analysis is divided into demographic and political determinants of support for each of the presidential candidate spouses. Also consistent with Chap. 3, there are three multivariate models presented in each table in order to address the challenge of multicollinearity problems between partisanship, ideology, and support of presidential candidates being included in a full model specification. Figure 4.4 displays the bivariate analyses of the mean feeling

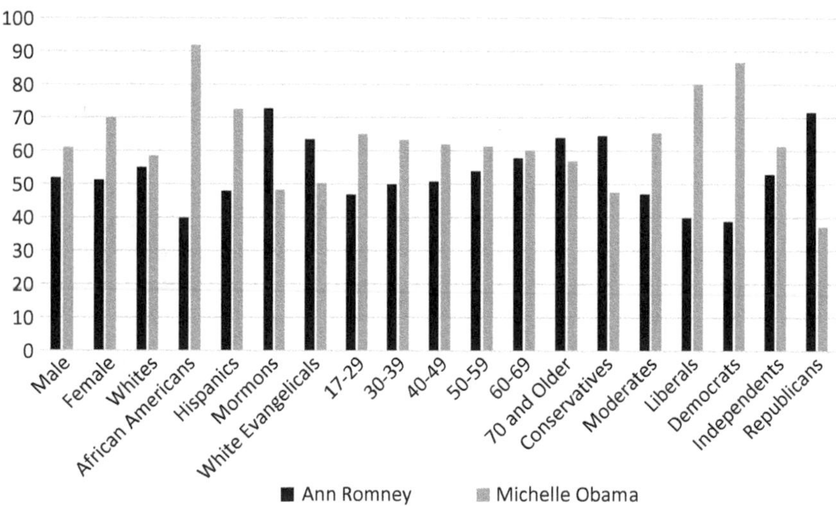

Fig. 4.4 Mean feeling thermometer ratings for Michelle Obama and Ann Romney among demographic and political groups from 2012 ANES

thermometer ratings for Michelle Obama and Ann Romney, while Tables 4.2 and 4.3 display the results from the multivariate regression analyses predicting support for each spouse.

Race and Ethnicity

Drawing on the theoretical framework of symbolic representation, this chapter argues that "historic firsts" Michelle Obama and Ann Romney should have special appeal to groups of citizens that they represent descriptively, who will rate them more favorably than other Americans. As the first African American woman to serve as first lady, Michelle Obama should generate higher levels of support among this group than among White

Table 4.2 Regression models predicting respondents' feeling thermometer rating of Michelle Obama's 2012 election

Independent variable	*Model 1*	*Model 2*	*Model 3*
Demographics			
Age	−0.025 (0.015)	−0.036 (0.021)	−0.015 (0.014)
Education	0.047 (0.027)	0.024 (0.037)	0.048 (0.065)
Income	0.070* (0.030)	0.031 (0.042)	0.083* (0.029)
Black	1.769* (0.770)	12.438* (1.060)	1.793* (0.726)
Hispanic	−1.499* (0.691)	3.803* (0.965)	−1.966* (0.003)
Female	2.312* (0.478)	2.759* (0.659)	2.445* (0.463)
Mormon	2.761 (1.907)	1.234 (2.682)	2.875 (1.885)
Born Again Evangelical	0.657 (0.532)	−0.558 (0.747)	0.555 (0.512)
Political variables			
Party ID (more Republican)	−0.467* (0.183)	−5.850* (0.227)	
Ideology (more conservative)	−0.111 (0.228)	−2.908* (0.313)	
Feeling thermometers			
Ann Romney	0.066* (0.015)	−0.120* (0.016)	0.062* (0.014)
Barack Obama	0.747* (0.012)		0.760* (0.010)
Mitt Romney	−0.069* (0.015)		−077* (0.014)
Mormons	−0.005 (0.012)	0.004 (0.017)	−0.008 (0.012)
Feminists	0.079* (0.012)	0.262* (0.016)	0.085* (0.011)
Blacks	0.057* (0.012)	0.185* (0.017)	0.054* (0.012)
Constant	12.877* (1.782)	75.072* (2.121)	9.841* (1.344)
Adjusted R^2	0.777	0.559	0.776
N	4482	4482	4731

Note: Parameter estimates are unstandardized regression coefficients, with standard errors in parentheses. Data are from the 2012 ANES

$^*p < 0.05$

Table 4.3 Regression models predicting respondents' feeling thermometer rating of Ann Romney's 2012 election

Independent variable	*Model 1*	*Model 2*	*Model 3*
Demographics			
Age	0.107* (0.016)	0.165* (0.019)	0.108* (0.015)
Education	0.007 (0.028)	−0.003 (0.035)	0.012 (0.028)
Income	0.043 (0.032)	0.077 (0.040)	0.047 (0.031)
Black	1.252 (0.825)	−1.105 (1.014)	0.821 (0.771)
Hispanic	−0.420 (0.732)	0.253 (0.911)	−0.606 (0.704)
Female	0.054 (0.507)	1.401* (0.634)	0.006 (0.493)
Mormon	−2.828 (2.020)	0.049 (2.530)	−2.403 (2.001)
Born Again Evangelical	1.013 (0.563)	3.091* (0.703)	1.342* (0.543)
Political variables			
Party ID (more Republican)	0.323 (0.194)	3.580* (0.223)	
Ideology (more conservative)	0.728* (0.241)	3.283* (0.294)	
Feeling thermometers			
Michelle Obama	0.074* (0.016)	−0.107* (0.0014)	0.069* (0.015)
Barack Obama	−0.080* (0.017)		−0.099* (0.016)
Mitt Romney	0.606* (0.012)		0.618* (0.011)
Mormons	0.159* (0.013)	0.322* (0.015)	0.163* (0.012)
Feminists	0.025* (0.012)	0.061* (0.015)	0.020 (0.12)
Blacks	0.055* (013)	0.055* (0.016)	0.053* (0.012)
Constant	0.775 (1.898)	−1.332 (2.263)	5.666* (1.433)
Adjusted R^2	0.630	0.419	0.625
N	4482	4483	4731

Note: Parameter estimates are unstandardized regression coefficients with standard errors in parentheses. Data are from the 2012 ANES

*$p < 0.05$

Americans. Race remains one of the most powerful predictors of political attitudes in the current political era (Ansolabehere et al. 2012). Over the past two generations African American voters have supported Democratic candidates in overwhelming numbers. Barack Obama's candidacies in 2008 and 2012 further strengthened that pattern (Sides and Vavreck 2013), signaling the importance of descriptive representation to people of color. The Republican Party's lack of support among African Americans should in turn translate into less favorable views of Ann Romney from Black respondents. While not as lopsided as the margins among African American voters, Democratic presidential candidates have tended to perform well among Hispanics in recent elections as well (Barreto and Segura 2014; Sides and Vavreck 2013; Wallace 2012). Hence, we expect to see the same pattern emerge for evaluations of Ann Romney and Michelle Obama among Hispanic voters.

Indeed, these expectations are borne out in both the bivariate and multivariate analyses. Michelle Obama was extraordinarily popular in 2012, with African Americans registering a mean feeling thermometer rating of 92 degrees. This near universal support among the African American community illustrates that even though they are not elected office holders, the visibility of first ladies can make them powerful symbolic figures for historically marginalized groups. Of course, much of this popularity can be attributed to her status as a major Democratic Party figure, which would tend to increase her popularity among African Americans. However, unlike with Hillary Clinton in 1992, in all three of the multivariate models Michelle Obama was perceived more favorably by African Americans even after controlling for major demographic and political variables ($p < 0.05$). Given the historic nature of the Obamas being the first Black Americans in the White House, it is perhaps not surprising to see that even after partisanship, ideology, and feelings toward Barack Obama are controlled, African Americans feel more warmly toward Michelle Obama than other Americans. To place these results in a historical context, however, it is interesting to note that African Americans did not view the previous two Democratic candidate spouses, Tipper Gore or Teresa Heinz Kerry, more positively compared to White Americans or Hispanic Americans (Burrell, Elder, and Frederick 2011). Thus, the results support the idea that the presence of Michelle Obama in the presidential campaign held particular symbolic importance among Black Americans, underscoring the value and impact of symbolic representation.

Also important to note is that in addition to this record-setting support among African Americans, Michelle Obama managed to maintain a positive image among Whites, with a mean feeling thermometer rating of 59 degrees. This cross-racial appeal is remarkable considering how so many issues divide White and Black Americans in contemporary society.

Michelle Obama was also highly popular among Hispanics, but it appears most of this support was driven by the fact that she was President Barack Obama's spouse. Her mean feeling thermometer rating among Hispanics was 73 degrees. Excluding evaluations of President Obama from the multivariate regression model, she was 4 degrees more popular among Hispanics compared to non-Hispanics ($p < 0.05$). However, in two of the three models including evaluations of Barack Obama, Hispanics rated her about 2 degrees less favorably after controlling for other political and demographic variables ($p < 0.05$). Michelle Obama was viewed quite favorably by Hispanics in 2012, but she did not experience the same kind of independent symbolic support she achieved among African Americans.

As anticipated, Ann Romney did not enjoy the same widespread cross-racial appeal that Michelle Obama did during the 2012 election. She was actually less popular among Whites than Michelle Obama, with a mean feeling thermometer rating of 55 degrees. She was even less popular among African Americans and Hispanics, with average ratings of 40 and 48 degrees, respectively. Nevertheless, these are not terrible ratings for a national Republican figure among people of color. For the sake of comparison, Mitt Romney had a mean rating of 41 degrees among Hispanics and 28 degrees among African Americans. Additionally, the relationships between race and ethnicity and support for Ann Romney were not statistically significant at conventional levels in any of the three multivariate models. Most of her low ratings among people of color were because of her associations with the Republican Party, and she was able to rise above that label to some degree.

In order to supplement this racial demographic analysis of support for the 2012 presidential candidate spouses, the multivariate analyses in this chapter also incorporate an affective measure of feelings about African Americans. Attitudes toward racial equality were a predominant factor in shaping political attitudes during President Obama's tenure on the national political scene (Kinder and Dale-Riddle 2012; Tesler 2016; Tesler and Sears 2010). Previous research has revealed that individuals with more negative attitudes toward African Americans feel less favorably toward Michelle Obama (Elder and Frederick 2017; Knuckey and Kim 2016). While many studies employ an index of survey items to capture racial resentment, the models presented in this chapter use the feeling thermometer rating about African Americans in each model specification. The primary reason for this usage is because it is measured on the same scale as the dependent variable and makes for an easy one-to-one interpretation of the substantive impact of the relationship.

The results confirm the findings of the earlier studies examining support for Michelle Obama. In all the three models, more negative views of African Americans are associated with more negative views of Michelle Obama. These results are consistent with the idea that racial resentment and/or racial prejudice act as a constraint on Michelle Obama's popularity and help explain why, even though she was viewed very warmly, she was not able to reach the heights of popularity achieved by Barbara Bush and

Laura Bush. More surprising is that negative views of African Americans are associated also with negative views of Ann Romney. This relationship is somewhat unexpected given that racial resentment and negative attitudes toward Black Americans are often a predictor of more support for Republican presidential candidates (Kinder and Dale-Riddle 2012; Knuckey 2011; Tesler 2016). This result illustrates how candidate spouses are able to carve out images in the public's mind that are distinctive from those of their party more generally.

Religion

Mitt Romney broke through a major religious barrier in 2012 when he became the first Mormon to be nominated by a major political party in the United States. Just as Michelle Obama galvanized unprecedented popularity in the African American community, the possibility that Ann Romney could have become first lady would have represented a major symbolic breakthrough for adherents of the Mormon faith potentially generating higher levels of support from this demographic group. The ANES data in Fig. 4.3 confirm this expectation, as the mean feeling thermometer rating for Ann Romney among Mormons was 73 degrees. This rating constituted her highest level of support from any of the groups examined. However, this relationship is not statistically significant once controls for other variables are accounted for in all the three multivariate models. Given the small sample of Mormons in the 2012 ANES, caution is warranted in assuming that she did not draw greater support among this group.[1] That said, Ann Romney's popularity among Mormons appears to be largely attributable to the fact that she was the spouse of the Republican presidential nominee among a demographic that overwhelmingly identifies with the Republican Party. The average feeling thermometer rating for Michelle Obama was 48 degrees among Mormons, which was her second lowest rating among the groups examined. Mormon identification was not a statistically significant predictor of support in any of the three multivariate models suggesting that Republican partisanship among Mormons was driving down her ratings with this group of voters.

For some Americans the idea of a Mormon first lady may not have been viewed so favorably. Previous research has demonstrated that the US public opinion toward the Mormon faith lags behind other religions (Penning 2009). With heightened attention on Mitt Romney's faith in the 2012 elections, affective reactions toward Mormons may have influenced perceptions of Ann Romney. The 2012 ANES included a feeling thermometer question asking how respondents felt about Mormons. This variable allows us to gauge the extent to which attitudes toward this group shaped evaluations of Ann Romney and Michelle Obama in the 2012 campaign. The results in Table 4.2 indicate that individuals with more positive views of Mormons also responded more favorably to Ann Romney, but on the flip side, anti-Mormon sentiment also significantly detracted from how warmly she was received by the public ($p < 0.05$). To the degree that religion influenced perceptions of spouses in the 2012 election, it did so in the form of people's overall feelings toward Mormons translating into their disposition toward Ann Romney. The feeling thermometer rating was not a statistically significant predictor of support for Michelle Obama in any of the three multivariate analyses.

The core of the base of the Republican Party over the past generation has come from Born Again Evangelical voters (Gold and Russell 2007; Layman 2001), yet there is a feeling among many evangelicals that Mormons are not genuine Christians and Mitt Romney had struggles appealing to this group in the 2008 and 2012 primaries (Campbell et al. 2012, 2016). Figure 4.3 demonstrates that despite her status as a Mormon, Ann Romney was fairly popular with White Evangelicals, earning a mean feeling thermometer rating of 63 degrees. In two of the three multivariate models, Evangelicals expressed a more positive evaluation of Ann Romney compared to other respondents ($p < 0.05$). Considering the decline of the Democratic Party's fortune among Born Again Evangelicals, it is not surprising that Michelle Obama's average feeling thermometer rating among White Evangelicals was much lower than the rating for Ann Romney. Michelle Obama's average feeling thermometer score among White Evangelicals was at neutral point of 50 degrees. Although White Evangelicals were responsible for one of her lowest ratings among the groups examined, this rating is fairly strong considering the Republican leaning nature of this demographic.

Gender and Feminism

Drawing on the theoretical framework of symbolic representation, gender is another demographic variable expected to influence support for the candidates' spouses. As discussed previously, presidential campaigns routinely employ spouses toward the objective of appealing to female voters. Moreover, candidate spouses are often one of the few and/or most visible women involved in presidential campaigns. Thus, there are reasons to expect women would feel a distinctively strong connection with candidate spouses. In comparison with Ann Romney, Michelle Obama should garner more support from women relative to men, consistent with the advantage Democratic politicians have with women in public opinion polls and most elections.

The results in Fig. 4.3 confirm the greater popularity of Michelle Obama among women, at 70 degrees, than men at 61 degrees. This result holds up but diminishes somewhat in the multivariate models. Across each model, even those that control for partisanship, ideology, and evaluations of Barack Obama, women evaluate Michelle Obama more favorably than do men ($p < 0.05$). While not a massive difference, this gap indicates that attitudes toward her were gendered, and that women were particularly drawn to her. Michelle Obama was one of the most visible women in the male-dominated world of presidential politics, and like many first ladies before her, Michelle Obama gave voice to the concerns and perspectives of women, offering them a type of representation and sense of connection to the political process that male presidential candidates have not (Borrelli 2011; Mansbridge 1999), and in return women viewed her more favorably.

Unlike evaluations of Michelle Obama, men rated Ann Romney slightly higher than women, 52 degrees to 51 degrees, although the difference was not statistically significant at the 0.05 level. Additionally, in two of the three multivariate models, the relationship between gender and support for Ann Romney is not statistically significant, confirming the bivariate results that there was no gender gap in her evaluations. These results suggest that despite her concerted effort to appeal to women voters, including her "I love you women" shout-out during her 2012 Republican Convention speech, she was evaluated no more favorably by women than she was by men (Elder and Frederick 2017). On the other hand, women were not particularly negative toward Ann Romney either. Most Republican candidates perform particularly poorly among women, and for Ann Romney this was not the case. Thus, Ann Romney was able to neutralize the Republican Party's typical deficit with women.

As was documented in Chap. 3, views about the role of women in society may also play a role in explaining support for the presidential candidate spouses in the context of the 2012 elections. Feelings toward feminism have been documented to influence a variety of political attitudes (Schnittker et al. 2003). In Chap. 3, pro-feminist attitudes were positively related to support for Hillary Clinton in the 1992 election suggesting that she offered symbolic representation to those seeking gender equality. The 2012 ANES also included a feeling thermometer survey question probing respondents' attitudes toward feminists, which is incorporated into the models predicting support for Michelle Obama and Ann Romney. Although the impact should not be as strong as it was for Hillary Clinton in 1992 given the untraditional or feminist way Hillary Clinton approached the role of candidate spouse in 1992 compared to the more traditional approach of Michelle Obama and Ann Romney, there is reason to expect that individuals with more favorable views of feminists should hold more favorable views toward Michelle Obama given her accomplished career history and her modern and autonomous style of self-presentation (Cottle 2012) and less toward Ann Romney whose life choices were more consistent with traditional expectations for women.

The results in Table 4.2 corroborate that more favorable attitudes toward feminists have a positive and statistically significant impact on support for Michelle Obama in all the three models ($p < 0.05$). Thus, not only did Michelle Obama garner particularly warm reactions from women, but also from those who support the political movement for gender equality. Somewhat unexpectedly, the affective assessments of feminists are also statistically significant predictors of support for Ann Romney in all but one model specification ($p < 0.05$). While she may not have appealed to women any more than she appealed to men, Ann Romney did engender greater support among voters with greater affinity toward feminism.

Age and Feelings Toward Ann Romney and Michelle Obama

The final demographic variable of interest in the 2012 election is age. Recent US elections have been characterized by an increasing generational divide, with younger voters supporting the Democratic Party in greater numbers and older voters leaning more heavily toward Republicans. Widespread support among young people was a vital part of Barack Obama' successful electoral coalitions in 2008 and 2012 (Sides and Vavreck 2013). Moreover, Chap. 3 showed that older voters were particularly supportive of Republican presidential spouse Barbara Bush, suggesting that her traditional approach to the role was particularly appealing to older generations. The data in Fig. 4.3 confirm that age is indeed related to perceptions of Ann Romney. She receives her highest average rating (65 degrees) among individuals over 70 years old and her lowest average rating of 47 degrees among individuals aged 17–29 years. The multivariate model bolsters this finding as age is positively related to support for Ann Romney in all the three models ($p < 0.05$). These results add further support to the idea that older Americans are particularly drawn to presidential spouses embodying traditional roles.

Michelle Obama is most popular among young people, with an average rating of 65 degrees, and least popular among individuals aged 70 and older, with an average rating of 57 degrees. However, with positive ratings across all generations, Michelle Obama's support transcended age in the 2012 election, a conclusion which is fortified by the multivariate analysis where age is not a statistically significant predictor of her support in any of the three models. While younger Americans found much to like in Michelle Obama, her decision to pursue a traditional role in terms of her actions as a presidential spouse seems to have also won over older generations as well.

Political Variables

In order to fully explore our theoretical frameworks concerning partisanship, ideology, and candidate evaluations, it is important to examine the role of political variables in shaping views toward Michelle Obama and Ann Romney. As discussed in the previous chapter, even popular first ladies such as Barbara Bush experienced some degree of partisan polarization in their support. However, between 1992 and 2012, partisan polarization expanded markedly (Campbell 2016), so this trend should also manifest itself in more polarized support for Michelle Obama and Ann Romney. The ANES data in Fig. 4.3 confirm this expectation. Michelle Obama was viewed very favorably by Democrats, with an average rating of 87 degrees, but far less positively by Republicans, with an average rating of 37. Ann Romney had an average rating of 72 degrees among Republicans, which is 15 degrees lower than Michelle Obama's rating among Democrats. Michelle Obama not only received higher support among her own partisans but also performed better among independents than Ann Romney, with a 61 to 53 advantage. However, Ann Romney maintained a rating of 39 degrees among Democrats, which is similar to Michelle Obama's rating among Republicans. While 37 and 39 percent support among the opposite party partisans is not high, it is somewhat impressive in the era of polarized politics.

Ideological divisions were also present in evaluations of the presidential candidate spouses in 2012, but they were not quite as stark as the partisan divide. Michele Obama averaged a rating of 80 degrees among liberals but still managed to garner an average rating of 48 degrees among conservatives. Ann Romney received an average rating of 65 among conservatives and an average rating of 40 degrees among liberals.

The results from the multivariate models largely support the bivariate results. The estimates for partisanship and ideology are both in the hypothesized direction, with more conservative respondents and respondents more strongly identifying with the Republican Party expressing less favorable views of Michelle Obama. Partisanship and ideology are strongly correlated with assessments of the president, and when those assessments are accounted for, the impact of party and ideology diminishes substantially. Excluding assessments of Barack Obama and Mitt Romney, the parameter estimate for party identification is −5.85. This estimate translates into a 35 degree difference in support between the strongest Democrat and the strongest Republican in their support for Michelle Obama. The value of the coefficient falls to −0.47 when the ratings of the candidates themselves are included in the model. The corresponding parameter estimates for ideology are −2.9 and −0.111, and in the full model, ideology is no longer a statistically significant predictor.

As was the case with Michelle Obama, evaluations of Ann Romney were influenced by partisanship and ideology, although the strength of this relationship was mediated by evaluations of the presidential candidates. In the model excluding Mitt Romney and Barack Obama, controlling for all the remaining independent variables, a one-unit shift in Republican identification leads to an increase of 3.6 degrees in the feeling thermometer rating of Ann Romney ($p < 0.05$). A one-unit shift in conservatism results in a 3.3 degree increase in Ann Romney's rating. Given the strong correlation with partisanship, once support for Mitt Romney and Barack Obama is accounted for, the size of the coefficients declines substantially and party identification is no longer statistically significant.

For both Ann Romney and Michelle Obama, evaluations of their spouses are the strongest predictors of support. In the two model specifications including President Obama's ratings, an additional one degree increase in support of President Obama results in an approximately 0.75 degree increase in the Michelle Obama's feeling thermometer score ($p < 0.05$). To better understand the magnitude of this result, the difference in Michelle Obama's rating between a respondent who rated

President Obama least favorably (zero) and a respondent who evaluated him the most favorably (100) is 75 degrees, all else equal.

Among the affective predictors of Ann Romney's favorability, Mitt Romney's feeling thermometer rating exerted the most powerful impact. For every one degree increase in Mitt Romney's rating, there is corresponding 0.60 degree increase in Ann Romney's rating ($p > 0.05$). To better understand the magnitude of this statistic, the difference in Ann Romney's rating between a respondent who rated Mitt Romney least favorably (zero) and a respondent who evaluated him the most favorably (100) is 60 degrees, all else equal.[2] Feelings toward her spouse strongly colored evaluations of Ann Romney, but not quite at the same magnitude as President Obama's ratings influenced evaluations of Michelle Obama. Similar to the findings in Chap. 3, feelings toward the candidate spouses in 2012 were strongly influenced by perceptions of the candidates themselves. However, there was also some degree of autonomy. Both Michelle Obama and Ann Romney were able to garner warmer feelings among opposite party partisans than their spouses, which help explains why they maintained high favorable ratings than their husbands. Evaluations of the opposing presidential candidates spouse were negative predictors of support for Michelle Obama and Ann Romney ($p < 0.05$). However, the magnitude of the effects was far smaller than it was for evaluations of the own spouses.

A final noteworthy finding concerns feelings toward the opposite spouse. In the model excluding the ratings of the presidential candidates (the second model in Table 4.2), evaluations of Ann Romney are negatively related to evaluations of Michelle Obama ($p < 0.05$). What these data suggest is that without Mitt Romney in model, some of the negative feelings toward him are spilling over and being picked up by Ann Romney. In other words, Ann Romney is acting as a proxy for feelings toward her husband. We believe that the first and third models in Table 4.2, where feelings toward the presidential candidates are controlled for, are a better reflection of what is actually going on. Those who view Mitt Romney warmly are not surprisingly more likely to view Michelle Obama unfavorably. But once feelings for Mitt Romney are controlled for, there is a positive relationship between feelings toward Michelle Obama and Ann Romney ($p < 0.05$). Positive feelings toward Ann Romney predict positive feelings toward Michelle Obama, and vice versa (see Tables 4.2 and 4.3). These results indicate that many Americans hold a reserve of warmth or perhaps sympathy for presidential candidate spouses regardless of party. The major takeaway here is that once feelings toward the presidential candidates are properly controlled for, individuals are more positively (or negatively) inclined toward the spouses of presidential candidates independent of other factors.

Discussion and Conclusion

The 2012 election featured two presidential candidate spouses who broke through historical barriers of race and religion. Despite their historically unconventional public profiles, both Michelle Obama and Ann Romney behaved in ways consistent with the theory of new traditionalism—actively campaigning for their husbands, while embracing traditionally gendered roles and steering clear of major policy influence—and as a result, Americans viewed both spouses quite favorably.

In 2008, Michelle Obama received favorability ratings that were on par with other non-incumbent presidential spouses. However, after serving for four years as first lady, she used the institutional advantages that come with the office to enhance her personal standing in the eyes of the public even further. Just as presidents exploit the perquisites of office to increase their electoral fortunes (Mayhew 2008), Michelle Obama showed, as Barbara Bush before her, that sitting first ladies can also effectively replicate this approach to boost their own popularity provided they do so within the parameters of public expectations. Indeed, much of Michelle Obama's personal popularity appears to be the result of her decision to operate carefully within the realm of new traditionalism. While Michelle Obama was of the most active first ladies in terms of public appearances and campaigning for her husband (Wright 2016), she also gave up her own career to support her husband's political ambitions, proclaimed that her most important job was being "mom-in-chief," and pursued projects such as the "Let's Move!" health campaign for children and the initiative to help veterans and military families, that are comfortably within the sphere of traditionally appropriate issues for a first lady (Hayden 2017; Guerrero 2011; Kahl 2009; Vigil 2014). In direct contrast to Hillary Clinton in the early 1990s, who openly played a major role crafting health care policy in her husband's administration, Michelle Obama played a hands-off policy role. Thus, even though Michelle Obama challenged the traditional image of presidential candidate spouses through her race and to some degree her modern, autonomous personality, she was able to amass a significant incumbency advantage due to her decision to behave in a traditional manner.

Ann Romney was less popular than Michelle Obama in 2012, but this standing in the eyes of the public had more to do with a lack of name recognition and non-incumbency disadvantage than her religion or any other factors that political observers in the news media have suggested. Ann Romney's average ratings were in line with most non-incumbent spouses and increased over the course of the 2012 campaign. Whether she could have enjoyed the same popularity as Michelle Obama if she had become first lady is conjecture, but her dutiful campaigning for her husband and a decision to pursue a traditional model of operation that did not challenge the gendered norms that characterize the position make it a distinct possibility that she also would have benefited from the incumbency advantage as well.

Another important theme emerging from our results is that, not surprisingly, the increasing polarization of the political sphere has indeed bled into evaluations of presidential candidate spouses to some degree. In most of the multivariate models presented in this chapter, party identification and ideology shape the public's perceptions of Michelle Obama and Ann Romney. Consistent with the theory of negative partisanship (Abramowitz and Webster 2016), the polarization of presidential candidate spouses is likely one of the drivers behind the relatively higher level of unfavorable ratings garnered by both Michelle Obama and Ann Romney in comparison to their predecessors (see Fig. 2.2 in Chap. 2). Increasing partisan polarization helps explain why Michelle Obama, while quite popular, did not manage to get the level of support among Republicans that Barbara Bush managed to achieve among Democrats. It is unlikely any presidential spouse going forward will be able to capture this level of support among adherents of the opposition party.

While there is no doubt that increased partisan polarization set limits on how high the favorable ratings of Michelle Obama and Ann Romney could go, at the same time, both Ann Romney and Michelle Obama were less polarizing and more popular figures than their husbands, thus underscoring the theme of independence in public evaluations of candidate spouses. While the individual-level results confirm that views of the presidential candidates exert influence on public opinion toward their spouses, this relationship does not preclude spouses from developing their own independent profiles that are distinct from their husbands. The fact that Michelle Obama was able to boast such high favorable ratings across the 2012 campaign, even after her husband had been in office for one full term, shows that presidential spouses still hold some ability to rise above the partisan fray and appeal to those outside the base of the party. Indeed, even though we found that Ann Romney was not viewed as positively as Michelle Obama, like most candidate spouses Ann Romney was popular, with favorable ratings far above her unfavorable ratings. Thus, 2012 continues a trend documented in past research that presidential candidate spouses retain a distinctive ability to remain above the partisan fray and cultivate a more popular image than their spouses, even in today's intensely partisan political terrain.

A couple of factors appear to be driving Michelle Obama's and Ann Romney's ability to retain higher than expected levels of support among opposite party partisans and remain more popular than their husbands. The first is their embrace of new traditionalism. By emphasizing traditionally feminine roles and issues, while also being a highly visible presence on the campaign trail, Michelle Obama and Ann Romney were able to generate not only high levels of support from their own partisans, but also more favorable responses among groups not typically disposed to like Democratic or Republican national political figures. Another explanation for the relative popularity of the 2012 candidate spouses may be the sense among a significant minority of Americans that presidential candidate spouses should be viewed with more sympathy than other people campaigning on behalf of presidential candidates (Gfk Omni survey 2017). It is important to reiterate that when perceptions of the presidential candidates were controlled for, attitudes toward Ann Romney predicted positive attitudes toward Michelle Obama and vice versa. This is consistent with the idea that there are Americans who liked and supported both of these candidate spouses, regardless of partisanship, ideology, and attitudes toward their husbands. It seems likely that Americans hold a reserve of warmth or perhaps sympathy for these women who must endure the intense scrutiny of a presidential campaign even though they themselves have not chosen to run for office. We saw a similar pattern Chap. 3, with evaluations of Barbara Bush and Hillary Clinton.

Another major takeaway from this chapter is the confirmation that the spouses of the presidential candidates can be symbolic representatives for members of groups that have historically been excluded from the political process in the United States. Ann Romney's strong support among adherents to the Mormon faith demonstrates the power of symbolic representation in public evaluations of presidential candidate spouses. Mormons gave her the highest feeling thermometer rating of all the groups included in the analysis, although this relationship was largely influenced by views of Mitt Romney who was the first Mormon presidential candidate nominated by one of the two major US political parties.

No presidential candidate embodies the phenomenon of symbolic representation better than Michelle Obama and her connection to the African American community and to women. The results reviewed in this chapter suggest that during the 2012 election, Michelle Obama provided a particularly meaningful form of representation to groups she descriptively represented and who have historically had very little representation within the realm of presidential politics and presidential administrations—women and African Americans—and in return these groups viewed her particularly favorably. Given her four years on the national stage as first lady, Michelle Obama in 2012 was one of the most visible women in the male-dominated world of presidential politics. Michelle Obama also gave voice to the concerns and perspectives of women, offering them a type of representation and sense of connection to the political process that male presidential candidates have not (Borrelli 2011; Mansbridge 1999), and in return women viewed her more favorably.

Even more powerful, Michelle Obama's ascendancy to the position of first lady was a signal to African Americans just how far racial progress had come, and they rewarded her with ratings even higher than Barack Obama. The fact that Michelle Obama managed to capture universal acclaim among African Americans, as she enjoyed strong ratings during a time of increased racial polarization (Abramowitz 2017; Czaja et al. 2015; Kinder and Dale-Riddle 2012; Tesler 2016; Tesler and Sears 2010), was a remarkable accomplishment. Of course, she was not immune from racial prejudice, as the analyses showed individuals with negative attitudes toward African Americans viewed her more unfavorably than individuals with positive views of African Americans. The broad acceptance by the American people of a woman of color in the role of first lady is important; it is something that was most likely unthinkable just a few decades previous. While future public opinion polls will be needed to offer a more robust test of the impact on public opinion, it seems likely to have altered and broadened what a first lady can look like in the eyes of Americans, especially American children, the focus of so much of first lady Michelle Obama's advocacy and outreach.

Notes

1. The 2012 ANES included a total of 82 Mormon respondents, which constituted 1.4 percent of the total sample.
2. Compare that estimate to the impact of partisanship in the model excluding the evaluations of the spouses. Controlling for all the other variables in the model, strong Republicans (maximum value) evaluate Ann Romney 25.2 degrees more favorably than strong Democrats (minimum value).

Bibliography

Abramowitz, Alan I. 2011. *The Disappearing Center: Engaged Citizens, Polarization and American Democracy*. New Haven, CT: Yale University Press.

———. 2017. It Wasn't the Economy Stupid, White Racial Resentment, and the Rise of Trump. In *Trumped the Election that Broke All of the Rules*, ed. Larry J. Sabato, Kyle Kondik, and Geoffrey Skelly, 202–210. Lanham, MD: Rowman and Littlefield.

Abramowitz, Alan I., and Stephen Webster. 2016. The Rise of Negative Partisanship and the Nationalization of U.S. Elections in the 21st Century. *Electoral Studies* 41 (1): 12–22.

Ansolabehere, Stephen, Nathaniel Persily, and Charles Stewart III. 2012. Regional Differences in Racial Polarization in the 2012 Presidential Election: Implications for the Constitutionality of Section 5 of the Voting Rights Act. *Harvard Law Review* 126: 205–220.

Barreto, Matt, and Gary Segura. 2014. *Latino America: How America's Most Dynamic Population is Poised to Transform the Politics of the Nation*. New York: Public Affairs Books.

Borrelli, Maryanne. 2011. *The Politics of the President's Wife*. College Station, TX: Texas A&M University Press.

Burrell, Barbara, Laurel Elder, and Brian Frederick. 2011. From Hillary to Michelle: Public Opinion and the Spouses of Presidential Candidates. *Presidential Studies Quarterly* 41 (1): 156–176.

Campbell, James E. 2016. *Polarized: Making Sense of a Divided America*. Princeton, NJ: Princeton University Press.

Campbell, David E., John C. Green, and J. Quin Monson. 2012. The Stained Glass Ceiling: Social Contact and Mitt Romney's 'Religion Problem'. *Political Behavior* 34 (2): 277–300.

———. 2016. *Seeking the Promised Land: Mormons and American Politics*. New York: Cambridge University Press.

Caroli, Betty Boyd. 2010. *First Ladies: From Martha Washington to Michelle Obama*. Oxford: Oxford University Press.

Cottle, Michelle. 2012. Battle of the First Ladies: Michelle Obama vs. Ann Romney. *Newsweek*, November 9. Accessed July 22, 2015. http://www.newsweek.com/battle-first-ladies-michelle-obama-vs-ann-romney-63859

Craighill, Peyton, and Erin Eastabrooks. 2012. Voters Prefer Michelle Obama and Ann Romney to Their Husbands. *Washington Post*, October 10. Accessed July 22, 2015.

Czaja, Erica, Jane June, and Tali Mendelberg. 2015. Race, Ethnicity and the Group Bases of Public Opinion. In *New Directions in Public Opinion*, ed. Adam Berinsky, 2nd ed., 104–123. New York: Routledge.

Davidson, Amy. 2012. Love and Presidents: The Difference Between Michelle and Ann. *The New Yorker*, September 5. Accessed July 22, 2015. http://www.newyorker.com/news/daily-comment/love-and-presidents-the-difference-between-michelle-and-ann

Duerst-Lahti, Georgia. 2014. Presidential Elections: Gendered Space and the Case of 2012. In *Gender and Elections: Shaping the Future of American Politics*, ed. Susan J. Carroll and Richard L. Fox, 3rd ed., 16–48. Cambridge: Cambridge University Press.

Elder, Laurel, and Brian Frederick. 2017. Perceptions of Candidate Spouses in the 2012 Presidential Election: The Role of Gender, Race, Religion, and Partisanship. *Politics, Groups, and Identities*. https://doi.org/10.1080/21565503.2017.1338969

Elder, Laurel, and Steven Greene. 2016. The Politics of Walmart Moms: Parenthood and Political Attitudes in the 2012 Election. *Journal of Women, Politics & Policy* 37 (4): 369–393.

Gfk Omni Survey. 2017. KnowledgePanel (KP) OmniWeb Survey Conducted by Gfk Custom Research LLC, September 15–17.

Gold, Howard J., and Gina E. Russell. 2007. The Rising Influence of Evangelicalism in American Political Behavior, 1980–2004. *The Social Science Journal* 44: 554–562.

Griffin, Farah Jasmine. 2011. At Last…? Michelle Obama, Beyonce, Race and History. *Daedalus* 140 (1): 141–151.

Groer, Annie. 2012. Michelle Obama and Ann Romney: Compare and Contrast. *The Washington Post*, October 21. Accessed July 20, 2015.

Guerrero, Lisa. 2011. (M)Other-in-Chief: Michelle Obama and the Ideal of Republican Womanhood. In *New Femininities*, ed. R. Gill and C. Scharff, 68–82. London: Palgrave Macmillan.

Hayden, Sara. 2017. Michelle Obama, Mom-in-Chief: The Racialized Contexts of Maternity. *Women's Studies in Communication* 40 (1): 11–28.

Kahl, Mary L. 2009. First Lady Michelle Obama: Advocate for Strong Families. *Communication and Critical Studies* 6 (3): 316–320.

Kinder, Donald R., and Allison Dale-Riddle. 2012. *The End of Race? Obama and Racial Politics in America*. New Haven, CT: Yale University Press.

Knuckey, Jonathan. 2011. Racial Resentment and Vote Choice in the 2008 Presidential Election. *Politics and Policy* 39: 559–582.

Knuckey, Jonathan, and Myunghee Kim. 2016. Evaluations of Michelle Obama as First Lady: The Role Racial Resentment. *Presidential Studies Quarterly* 46 (2): 365–386.

Kucinich, Jackie, and Martha T. Moore. 2012. Hilary Clinton Says Ann Romney Never Worked 'Day in Her Life'. *USA Today*, April 12. Accessed June 20, 2016. http://usatoday30.usatoday.com/news/politics/story/2012-04-12/ann-romney-hilary-rosen-work/54235706/1

Layman, Geoffrey. 2001. *The Great Divide: Religious and Cultural Conflict in American Politics*. New York: Columbia University Press.

Mansbridge, Jane. 1999. Should Blacks Represent Blacks and Women Represent Women? *Journal of Politics* 61: 628–657.

Mayhew, David R. 2008. Incumbency Advantage in U.S. Presidential Elections: The Historical Record. *Presidential Studies Quarterly* 123 (2): 201–228.

Parks, Gregory S., and Quinetta M. Roberson. 2009. Michelle Obama: A Contemporary Analysis of Race and Gender through the Lens of Title IX. *Hastings Women's Law Journal* 20 (1): 3–44.

Penning, James M. 2009. Americans' Views of Muslims and Mormons: A Social Identity Theory Approach. *Politics and Religion* 2 (2): 277–302.

Schnittker, Jason S., Jeremy Freese, and Brian Powell. 2003. Who Are Feminists and What Do They Believe? The Role of Generations. *American Sociological Review* 68 (4): 607–622.

Sides, John, and Lynn Vavreck. 2013. *The Gamble: Choice and Chance in the 2012 Presidential Election*. Princeton, NJ: Princeton University Press.

Tesler, Michael. 2016. *Post-Racial or Most-Racial?* Chicago: Chicago University Press.

Tesler, Michael, and David O. Sears. 2010. *Obama's Race: The 2008 Election and the Dream of a Post-Racial America*. Chicago: Chicago University Press.

Vigil, Tammy R. 2014. Feminine Views in the Feminine Style: Convention Speeches by Presidential Nominees' Spouses. *Southern Communication Journal* 79: 327–346.

Von Drehle, David. 2012. The Ascent of Ann Romney. *Time*, August 28, 2012. http://swampland.time.com/2012/08/28/the-ascent-of-ann-romney/

Wallace, Sophia. 2012. It's Complicated: Latinos, President Obama, and the 2012 Election. *Social Science Quarterly* 93: 1360–1383.

Wright, Lauren. 2016. *On Behalf of the President: Presidential Spouses and White House Communications Strategy Today*. Santa Barbara, CA: Praeger.

CHAPTER 5

Breaking with the Past: Public Opinion Toward Melania Trump and Bill Clinton in the 2016 Election

The 2016 presidential campaign turned many conventional expectations and much of the academic scholarship about presidential candidate spouses on its head. As Chap. 2 reveals, Melania Trump and Bill Clinton made history as the most unpopular candidate spouses from 1988, when pollsters began collecting this data, through the present. Melania Trump invoked a particularly negative reaction from the public. Over the course of the 2016 election, she had the lowest favorable average of all candidate spouses. Notably, she is the only spouse in modern history that suffered from higher unfavorable ratings than favorable ratings, which is particularly striking given her newness to the national political stage. While Bill Clinton also had high unfavorable ratings, making him the second least popular candidate spouse after Melania Trump (see Fig. 2.3 in Chap. 2), his high unfavorable ratings were coupled with relatively high favorable ratings. Generating such a polarized response from the public is also unusual among presidential candidate spouses.

Melania Trump and Bill Clinton also departed from the typical script for presidential candidate spouses, although each in unique ways. In addition to the fact that she would ultimately become the first foreign-born first lady since Louisa Adams in the 1820s (Caroli 2010), Melania Trump was distinctive for her near invisibility on the campaign trail (Ioffe 2016; Wright 2017), earning headlines such as "The Silent Partner" (Trebay 2015). In contrast, Bill Clinton, as a former two-term president of the United States, carried near universal name recognition and a well-known

L. Elder et al., *American Presidential Candidate Spouses*,
https://doi.org/10.1007/978-3-319-73879-6_5

political record. He was also the first man to take on the role of major party presidential candidate spouse, thereby flipping the script on the highly feminized position of presidential candidate spouse.

This chapter analyzes public perceptions of the 2016 presidential candidate spouses, paying particular attention to how the public reacted to the non-traditional aspects of Bill Clinton's and Melania Trump's performances and images as presidential candidate spouses. It draws on a survey conducted by CNN in October 2016, as well as aggregate survey results, to better understand Americans' unusually negative evaluations of Bill Clinton and Melania Trump. The results reinforce themes developed in earlier chapters as well as offer new insights. While increasing partisan polarization and the historic unpopularity of the 2016 presidential candidates, Hillary Clinton and Donald Trump, contributed to the public's low opinion of Bill Clinton and Melania Trump, the inability of these two candidate spouses to conform to the expectations of new traditionalism (or their choice to defy these expectations) also drove their unpopularity. Unlike Michelle Obama and Ann Romney, the 2012 presidential candidate spouses, Melania Trump and Bill Clinton did not meet contemporary expectations for candidate spouses, and, as a result, they were not embraced as warmly by the public.

Bill Clinton, Melania Trump, and the Challenges of New Traditionalism

While Melania Trump did not speak at many campaign events, she did adopt a supportive, behind-the-scenes demeanor throughout the 2016 campaign that is in keeping with traditional expectations for presidential candidate spouses. In the few interviews she did during the campaign, Melania Trump made it clear that her first priority was being a mother and that politics and policy were her husband's job, not hers (Ioffe 2016). When Donald Trump introduced his wife for her first speaking campaign appearance, fairly late in the campaign season in April 2016, he said, "She's an incredible mother, she loves her son, Barron, so much. And I have to say, she will make an unbelievable First Lady" (Ioffe 2016). An emphasis on motherhood and a clear distance from policy has typically engendered a favorable view of candidate spouses among the public; this was not the case for Melania Trump.

One reason for this is that a number of unusual scandals emerged at various points during the campaign involving Melania Trump that challenged the traditional image of a first lady she seemed interested in presenting. Given that presidential candidate spouses receive intense media scrutiny, as well as the media's bias toward negative and scandalous stories, it is not uncommon for controversies related to candidate spouses to receive considerable attention in the news. The ones that emerged around Melania Trump, however, were unusual, centering on whether she worked without proper legal authorization when she first came to the United States as an immigrant; the use of nude photos of her from her former career as a model, as a campaign tactic by one of her husband's competitors; and her Republican Convention speech that was partially plagiarized from a speech First Lady Michelle Obama gave in 2008. While Melania Trump made it clear that she was interested in being a traditional candidate spouse, focused primarily on raising her son and supporting her husband from the sidelines, these scandals shaped an image of her that was much more controversial and complicated than that of a traditional first lady.

Another characteristic of Melania Trump that complicated her efforts to be seen as a traditional candidate spouse is her status as an immigrant. Melania Trump and Teresa Heinz Kerry, wife of the 2004 Democratic presidential nominee John Kerry, are the only two candidate spouses in the contemporary era (from 1988 to present) that are not native-born Americans. Teresa Heinz Kerry was born in colonial Mozambique (Thurman 2004), and Melania Trump was born in Slovenia when it was still a part of Yugoslavia. By default, the traditional or typical presidential candidate spouse has only been an American-born woman. It is also the case that Teresa Heinz Kerry, after Melania Trump and Bill Clinton, was one of the least well-liked candidate spouses (see Chap. 2). This raises the possibility that candidate spouses born outside the United States struggle to embody the "true American" image the public desires in the role of would-be first lady (Mandziuk 2017). Thus, despite Melania Trump's stated desire to present herself as a traditional wife, several aspects of her biography and performance as a candidate spouse defied traditional expectations for this role.

Importantly, Melania Trump's low favorability ratings appear to be a product of what she did not do. As 2017 survey data reveal (Fig. 2.1 in Chap. 2), a large majority of Americans think it is important for candidate spouses to be visible and active on the campaign trail on behalf of their husbands or wives. There is a sense that Americans are not only electing a president, but a first family, and therefore the public wants the opportunity to assess the familial ties of the candidate (Dittmar 2015). Moreover, the spouse offers the public unique, personal insights into the candidate that other campaign surrogates are simply not in a position to do (Wright 2016). Melania Trump violated this norm of modern campaigns. In contrast to her predecessors who headlined hundreds of campaign events as surrogates for their spouses (MacManus and Quecan 2008; Wright 2016), Melania Trump gave only a few speeches throughout the campaign (Wright 2017). As noted above, her first speaking role at a campaign event was not until April 2016, and after her controversial speech at the Republican Convention in July 2016, she was absent from the campaign trail until close to the election (Jordan and McCrummen 2016; Rappeport 2016).

By limiting her public appearances and dramatically limiting her speeches, Melania Trump not only defied contemporary expectations for presidential candidate spouses but also limited her ability to craft her own image and generate the soft news, feel-good media stories typical about candidate spouses. Melania Trump's relative absence from the campaign trail may have left her vulnerable to being defined by the scandals discussed previously, as well as defined even more than is usual by evaluations of her husband, a problem given that Donald Trump was the least popular of any presidential candidate in modern history. This latter possibility is explored in the individual-level analysis presented later in this chapter.

Despite being the first-ever male presidential candidate spouse, Bill Clinton worked hard to meet several of the key new traditionalism expectations for would-be first spouses. In contrast to Melania Trump, Bill Clinton pursued an active campaign schedule headlining close to 500 events on behalf of his wife's 2016 presidential bid (Horowitz 2016). Similar to other presidential campaigns over the past couple of decades, his wife's campaign strategically deployed Bill Clinton to build support among groups of voters seen as crucial to his wife's election. What distinguished him in this role was that rather than having him appeal to women voters, as most candidate spouses have been tasked with doing, Bill Clinton was sent to rural areas to appeal to White men (Horowitz 2016), earning him headlines like this one from *Politico*, asking "Can Bill Clinton win back the Bubba Vote?" (Karni 2016).

Additionally, in his campaign appearances, including his Democratic Convention speech, Bill Clinton took on another important role of modern candidate spouses, which is to humanize the candidate and to draw on personal and even intimate examples to make the case for why their spouse would be a good president. In his 2016 convention speech as well as campaign events across the nation, Bill Clinton spoke movingly about Hillary Clinton as a young woman, as a dedicated mother, and as a wife, with the goal of making her seem more relatable and likeable in the eyes of American voters.

Despite taking on the relentless campaign schedule and supporting role that has come to be expected of candidate spouses, Bill Clinton was anything but a traditional presidential candidate spouse. Bill Clinton was the first man to take on the role of major party presidential candidate spouse; thus, his very presence on the campaign trail challenged this traditionally feminized position. The American presidency is a strongly, some argue, hyper-masculinized role, and thus an implicit job of presidential candidate spouses has been to underscore the masculinity of their spouses (Borrelli 2011; Dittmar 2012; Duerst-Lahti 2014). Much attention during the 2016 campaign, therefore, focused on the apparent dissonance caused by a man seeking the title of "First Lady." News stories reflected Americans' fascination and amusement with the idea of a man assuming the role of first spouse. Story after story was written about what the first male presidential spouse should be called and what role he should play in the White House: should he be selecting China patterns or advising the president on economic policy (Fuller 2015; Merica 2015; Talbot 2016)? During one of the Democratic presidential debates, moderator Martha Raddatz asked Hillary Clinton whether it was time to change the role of presidential spouse away from responsibilities such as decorating the White House and hosting state dinners (Mandziuk 2017). Hillary Clinton indicated that she, not her husband, would likely take on those types of responsibilities.

In addition to being the first man to take on the role of presidential candidate spouse, Bill Clinton is also, obviously, a former two-term president of the United States and thus carried near universal name recognition and a well-known political record that could be both an asset and a liability. Given his experience, there was notable speculation in the media as well as discussion by Hillary Clinton herself of her husband acting as an economic policy adviser in her White House (Chozick 2016). Moreover, Bill Clinton's presidential past resurfaced as a campaign issue on multiple occasions throughout the presidential nomination process and the general election season. While polling organizations occasionally queried the public about Clinton's possible influence in a Hillary Clinton administration,

Table 5.1 Pollster inquiries about presidential candidate spouses during the 2016 campaign season

Poll questions asked about Melania Trump, 20

Favorability type questions (16): For example,

- Do you have a favorable or unfavorable view of Melania Trump?

Tailored questions (4)

- If Donald Trump wins the presidency, do you think Melania Trump would have a positive or negative impact on his presidency?
- Is it appropriate to publish nude pictures of Melania Trump as a way to attack Donald Trump?
- Is it appropriate for media to investigate whether or not Melania Trump violated federal immigration laws by working as a model in the United States before she obtained a proper work visa?
- How much does it bother you that parts of Melania Trump's speech were taken directly from Michelle Obama's speech in 2008?

Poll questions asked about Bill Clinton, 58

Favorability type questions (36)

Tailored questions (22)

- Questions about Bill Clinton's sexual transgressions (13): Who is more respectful of women, Bill Clinton or Donald Trump; How much does Bill Clinton respect women; Have Bill Clinton's sex scandals done more to help or hurt Hillary Clinton's career; Are Bill Clinton's sex scandals and/or treatment of women fair game/legitimate issue in 2016 campaign; does Bill Clinton's sexual past and way Hillary Clinton has dealt with it affect your vote; How much does it bother you that Hillary Clinton is accused of working to undermine the reputations of women linked to Bill Clinton's infidelity; How concerned are you about Hillary Clinton's criticisms of the women who accused Bill Clinton of inappropriate sexual behavior; do you think Hillary Clinton has or has not threatened to undermine women who have accused Bill Clinton of infidelity and sexual misconduct?
- Questions on Bill Clinton's influence on vote/spouse (5): Does Bill Clinton's involvement in Hillary Clinton's campaign make you more or less likely to support her? How enthusiastic or uncomfortable are you that Hillary Clinton is married to Bill Clinton? Would you prefer the Democratic nominee be Hillary Clinton or Bill Clinton? Will Bill Clinton have a positive or negative impact on Hillary Clinton's presidency? How much does it bother you that Bill Clinton will likely influence Hillary Clinton's decisions?
- Questions on the Clinton Foundation (3): Should Bill Clinton step down? How likely is it that Clintons were selling influence to foreign contributors who made donations to Clinton foundation? Should Clinton Foundation founded by Bill Clinton be shut down if Hillary is elected?
- Questions on health care (1): How closely have you followed stories about Bill Clinton's comments about Affordable Care Act

Source: Polls archived at the Roper Center for Public Opinion Research, January 1—Election Day 2016

the most common line of pollster inquiry concerned Bill Clinton's sexual transgressions (see Table 5.1), thereby underscoring the role of gender, masculinity, and the presidency in both old and new ways.

Attitudes Toward Melania Trump and Bill Clinton over the 2016 Campaign Season

In order to get a better sense of their overall standing in the minds of the American public, Figs. 5.1 and 5.2 draw on polling data archived at the Roper Center for Public Opinion Research to plot the favorable averages of Bill Clinton and Melania Trump from January 2016 through the general election in November. Figure 5.1 shows that Melania Trump began the campaign season not well-known to the American public. When pollsters asked Americans for their thoughts about her in February, May, and even mid-July of 2016, somewhere between 40 and 55 percent of Americans indicated that they did not know enough about her to offer an assessment.

The most high-profile campaign event concerning Melania Trump was her speech at the Republican Convention, which took place on July 18–21, 2016, in Cleveland, Ohio. Expectations for Melania Trump's speech were high because of Americans' fascination with candidate spouses and because

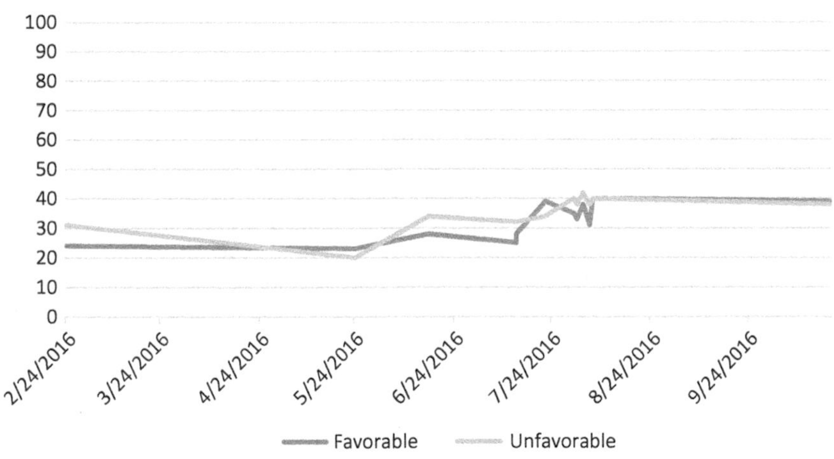

Fig. 5.1 Melania Trump's favorable/unfavorable ratings over the 2016 campaign

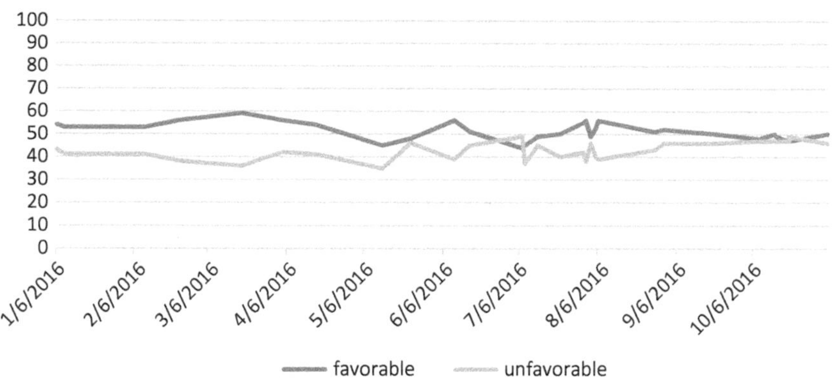

Fig. 5.2 Bill Clinton's favorable/unfavorable ratings over the 2016 campaign

she had played such a low-profile role during the campaign, and many saw this appearance as a chance to learn about her. While her speech was well-received in the convention hall among Republican loyalists, it was almost immediately engulfed in controversy when evidence surfaced that parts of the speech were plagiarized from a speech Michelle Obama had given in 2008 (Haberman and Barbaro 2016). *The Economist* and YouGov conducted a poll in the days following and found that reactions to the plagiarism controversy were steeply divided along partisan lines.[1] Of the 74 percent of Americans that had read or watched news about the convention, 58 percent were bothered a lot or a little that parts of Melania Trump's speech were plagiarized, yet Democrats and Republicans viewed the issue very differently. Consistent with the theory of negative partisanship, an incredible 90 percent of Democrats indicated that Melania Trump's plagiarism bothered them a lot or a little, whereas 67 percent of Republicans were not bothered at all. Clearly Democrats were using this incident as a means of expressing their overwhelming disapproval of the Republican Party and its presidential ticket. It is hard to believe that Democrats would be so unified in their concern over plagiarism in a speech former First Lady Barbara Bush delivered in a less politically polarized era.

While the Republican Convention raised Melania Trump's profile with the public, leading to a drop in the percentage of Americans who said they had no opinion of her, it did not change the favorable/unfavorable balance of her approval ratings. As opposed to other presidential candidate spouses for whom greater visibility has led to greater favorability (Burrell

2001; Saad 2016), Melania Trump's favorable and unfavorable ratings increased in lockstep. Thus, the Republican Convention was a missed opportunity for Melania Trump. Indeed, polls show that President Trump's daughter, Ivanka Trump, benefited from a bounce in her favorable ratings in the wake of her speech at the Republican Convention, which she retained for the remainder of the campaign (Reinhart 2017). One of the most striking takeaways from Fig. 5.1 is that unfavorable views of Melania Trump remained as high or higher than favorable views not just in the spring of 2016 when her husband, Donald Trump, was battling for the Republican nomination, but throughout the campaign, even through events such as the Convention that typically result in very positive coverage. The trend in Fig. 5.1 contrasts sharply with evaluations of Ann Romney over the course of the 2012 campaign shown in Chap. 4. As people got to know Ann Romney, most came to view her favorably. This was not the case for Melania Trump.

Figure 5.2 tracks evaluations of Bill Clinton over the course of the 2016 campaign. While both Bill Clinton and Melania Trump were characterized by unusually high unfavorable ratings, evaluations of these two spouses differed from one another in two important respects. First, unsurprisingly, Bill Clinton was well-known from the start. On average, only eight percent of Americans felt they could not offer an assessment of Bill Clinton, which is the lowest of any presidential candidate spouse. Such high levels of name recognition are not only a contrast to Melania Trump but are unprecedented for a non-incumbent presidential candidate spouse.

Second, Bill Clinton's strong unfavorable ratings were balanced out by even stronger favorable ratings. His favorable average across the campaign was 51 percent (shown in Chap. 2), which puts him fourth highest in the series after the incumbent first ladies Barbara Bush in 1992, Laura Bush in 2004, and Michelle Obama in 2012. The polarized reaction to Bill Clinton, with high favorable and high unfavorable averages, suggests that even though Bill Clinton carried out the typical responsibilities of contemporary candidate spouses, he was still being viewed through the polarized lens of partisanship typical of elected national leaders in the contemporary era. Such highly polarized evaluations are not typical of presidential candidate spouses or first ladies; however, such polarized evaluations are typical of well-known national political figures.

Bill Clinton's ratings were fairly steady early in the campaign season but declined a bit during the heated Democratic presidential nomination contest between Hillary Clinton and Bernie Sanders. This drop may have reflected controversy surrounding the negative coverage of the crime bill signed during his administration, as the Democratic presidential candidates expressed their desire to see less punitive criminal justice policies implemented (Berenson 2016). In contrast to Melania Trump, Bill Clinton appears to have benefited from a boost from his Democratic convention speech. As Election Day approached, however, his favorable ratings trended slightly downward once again. This negative trajectory is not surprising considering the media focus on his alleged sexual misconduct and his role in the Clinton foundation, which is discussed in more detail in the following section.

Pollster Inquiries

The number and nature of pollster inquiries about the candidate spouses across the 2016 campaign season (Table 5.1) also underscore how Melania Trump and Bill Clinton struggled to embody the traditional image and expectations the public has for candidate spouses. Given the ways Bill Clinton challenged the traditional role of candidate spouse, by being the first male spouse, by possessing his own prominent political career with a long history of scandal, and by engaging with the idea that he would be an adviser in a Hillary Clinton White House, it is not surprising that pollsters asked many more questions concerning Bill Clinton than Melania Trump—a total of 58 for Bill Clinton versus 20 for Melania Trump.[2] Bill Clinton's unprecedented political profile as a presidential spouse made him a magnet for political attention among the media in the 2016 campaign, and the polls reflected this reality. In fact, the only presidential candidate spouse in the modern era that pollsters asked about more often was Hillary Clinton in 1996, when pollsters queried the public repeatedly about her involvement in the Whitewater investigations as well as her involvement in her husband's administration.

There were only a handful of tailored questions about Melania, but tellingly these questions dealt with scandals, which underscored the ways she did not fit the traditional image of a candidate spouse. One of the first high-profile campaign issues to emerge surrounding Melania Trump related to her former career as a model. In March 2016, a super PAC supporting Republican presidential candidate Ted Cruz ran an advertisement in Utah featuring a nude photo of Melania Trump from a 2000 *GQ Magazine* photo shoot in an attempt to sway Republican voters, especially Mormons, against Trump in their state's Republican primary (Parker

2016). Donald Trump responded by tweeting an unflattering picture of Ted Cruz's wife next to a very flattering picture of his wife (Ioffe 2016; Parker 2016). This exchange, labeled by some news media outlets as "wifegate," spurred one polling firm to query Americans about whether they thought it was "appropriate or inappropriate to publish nude pictures of Melania Trump as a way to attack Donald Trump?" An overwhelming 77 percent thought this was inappropriate, including a majority of both Republicans and Democrats (YouGov 2016).

The wifegate scandal led the media to pay more attention to Melania Trump's former career as a model, and, in particular, whether she had legal working status when she began her modeling career in the United States (Ioffe 2016; Schreckinger and Debenedetti 2016). Stories continued to trickle out about this issue across the campaign, and in early November 2016, the AP finally offered documentation that Melania Trump did work ten modeling jobs before receiving legal work authorization (Caldwell et al. 2016). Pollsters asked about this issue in early August, and in contrast to the nude photos, more Americans (48 percent) found this to be a legitimate campaign issue compared to those that did not (35 percent) (YouGov 2016).

Besides one pollster question apiece about "wifegate," plagiarism, and her immigration status, there was only one other tailored question specifically about Melania Trump, a fairly standard question about her role as potential first lady and whether she would have a positive or negative impact on her husband's presidency. Unlike pollsters inquiries about Hillary Clinton in 1992 (see Chap. 3), there were no questions about Melania Trump's role as a potential policy adviser, her political ambition, whether she was too pushy, or whether she paid enough attention to her family. The lack of pollster inquiry on these topics reflects Melania Trump's clear signals that her interests as first lady would be quite traditional, focusing first and foremost on raising her son and that she had no interest in influencing policy in her husband's administration.

Table 5.1 also shows that the largest subset of tailored questions pollsters asked regarding Bill Clinton related to his marital infidelities when he served as president or governor of Arkansas and/or Hillary Clinton's reaction to those infidelities. Questions were asked about whether Bill Clinton respected women, whether his treatment of women was fair game in the election, and whether Hillary Clinton played a role in these scandals by criticizing the women accusers. It is notable that Bill Clinton's sexual transgressions were the only aspect of his presidential legacy that were asked about by pollsters during the 2016 election. Despite having a policy record on issues like crime and financial deregulation, which played prominent roles in the Democratic nomination contest in particular, media polling firms only focused on the scandalous and not the policy aspects of Bill Clinton's presidency.

There are a couple possible reasons that Bill Clinton's sex scandals became such a prominent theme in 2016 polling. One explanation is that Donald Trump pushed this storyline by raising the issue of Bill Clinton's infidelity and treatment of women multiple times, often in response to accusations about his own treatment of women. Prior to the New Hampshire primary, Donald Trump mentioned in speeches that Bill Clinton had a "penchant for sexism" and said Bill Clinton was "one of the great abusers of the world" (Mandziuk 2017). On Twitter on December 28, 2015, Donald Trump declared, "If Hillary thinks she can unleash her husband, with his terrible record of women abuse, while playing the women's card on me, she's wrong!" (Mandziuk 2017, 150). He went even further with this strategy in the general election by holding a news conference, just prior to his second presidential debate with Hillary Clinton, with three women who had accused Bill Clinton of sexual misconduct (Stack 2016). Donald Trump was exploiting Bill Clinton's history as a means of deflecting criticism of his own treatment of women following disclosure of an Access Hollywood video that captured him bragging about making unwanted sexual advances toward women. Considering the unorthodox and unprecedented nature of these events, the media chose to devote significant polling resources for gauging public reactions toward Bill Clinton's history in this area. Heightened attention to Bill Clinton's sexual transgressions may also be a cultural reaction to the gender-switching nature of Hillary Clinton's candidacy, where the nation was seeing for the first time a woman seeking the presidency and a male performing the role of would-be first candidate spouse. In this way, pollster inquiries and media coverage of Bill Clinton's sexual transgressions undermined Hillary Clinton's perceived legitimacy for the office of the presidency, in a similar manner as occurred during the 2008 Democratic presidential nomination contest (Dittmar 2012).

The other two themes to emerge from pollster inquiries about Bill Clinton concerned his possible influence in a Hillary Clinton administration and his role in the Clinton Foundation. Both of these lines of inquiry also reflected untraditional aspects of Bill Clinton's status as candidate spouse—his considerable political and policy influence, as well as possible conflicts of interest between the Clinton foundation and the US policy-making.

Individual-Level Analysis

The polling data reviewed above support the notion that neither Bill Clinton nor Melania Trump fit within the new traditional expectations for presidential candidate spouses, and in return the public viewed them unfavorably compared to previous candidate spouses. This section turns to individual-level analysis to further understand the public opinion toward Bill Clinton and Melania Trump, and to better understand the public's reaction to these two untraditional candidate spouses. What groups account for the distinctively low approval ratings of Melania Trump and to a lesser extent Bill Clinton? Is partisan polarization the driving cause? And to what extent was Melania Trump's exceptionally low favorable ratings a by-product of her husband's historically low favorable ratings? Were responses to Bill Clinton, the first male presidential candidate spouse, gendered in a new way?

CNN data from October 2016 are employed for this analysis as the American National Election Study, the source of data employed in the previous two chapters, did not ask a question about Melania Trump in 2016.[3] Similar to the two preceding chapters, two types of analyses are presented. The first is bivariate relationships between key independent variables—including gender, partisanship, and candidate evaluations—and the favorable averages of Melania Trump and Bill Clinton (the two preceding chapters displayed feeling thermometer ratings rather than favorable ratings). Figure 5.3 displays the average percentage of respondents in key demographic and political groups expressing a favorable view toward Melania Trump and Bill Clinton. It is important to keep in mind that more Americans were able to express an opinion toward Bill Clinton compared to Melania Trump, which acts to inflate his favorable averages compared to Melania Trump to some degree.

The second type of analysis presented is binary logistic regression models predicting whether individuals express favorable views of Bill Clinton and Melania Trump. These multivariate analyses allow for an assessment of whether relationships revealed in the bivariate analysis hold up after various control variables are introduced. The dependent variable in the models is coded 1 for individuals expressing a favorable opinion of each spouse and 0 otherwise. The predictor variables in each model include demographic variables such as age, education, and race as well as key political variables including partisanship, ideology, and attitudes toward the presidential candidates. Similar to previous chapters, three separate model

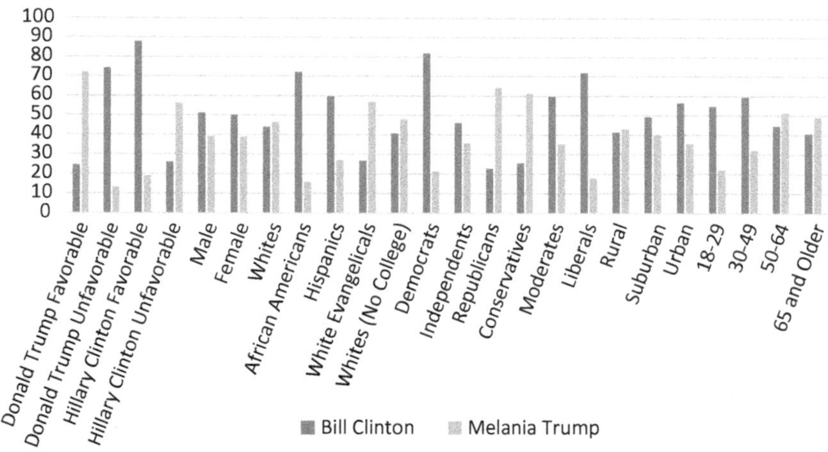

Fig. 5.3 Percent of respondents expressing a favorable opinion toward Bill Clinton and Melania Trump among demographic and political groups in the 2016 election

specifications for each spouse are presented, one including the presidential candidates' feeling thermometer rating, party identification, and ideology; one that excludes the presidential candidates' rating; and another that excludes party identification and ideology.

Gender

As discussed in previous chapters, candidate wives have often been dispatched to appeal to women voters, particularly given the importance of the gender gap in presidential elections. The results presented in Chaps. 3 and 4 show that women evaluate some presidential candidate spouses—most notably Barbara Bush and Michelle Obama—more favorably than men even when other factors are controlled, suggesting that women felt a sense of gender affinity with these candidate spouses. Given that candidate spouses are often one of the few or only women figures in the otherwise male-dominated presidential campaigns, they hold the potential to provide meaningful descriptive or symbolic representation to women and thus invoke a particularly favorable response.

Similar to previous candidate spouses, Melania Trump was deployed in her infrequent campaign appearances to appeal to women (Parker 2016), and she struck traditionally feminine and maternal themes in these appearances (Ioffe 2016; Mandziuk 2017; Wright 2017). In contrast, Bill Clinton was sent to small towns to appeal to rural White men (Horowitz 2016; Karni 2016).[4] Given the contrasting targets of their appeals, and Bill Clinton's status as the first male presidential candidate spouse, it is important to see if evaluations of Bill Clinton and Melania Trump are gendered, and if so, if they are gendered in-line with previous candidate spouses or in new ways.

The bivariate analyses presented in Fig. 5.3 show that Bill Clinton was slightly more popular among men than among women although this difference was not statistically significant. White men viewed him four percentage points more favorably than White women, and this difference was significant ($p < 0.05$). The fact that Bill Clinton received slightly more supportive evaluations from men deviates from the pattern of most Democratic Party political figures including prior candidate spouses and first ladies who generated higher ratings among women. The multivariate models presented in Table 5.2 also show that after controlling for other variables, no gender gap is present in favorability toward Bill Clinton. These non-effects, however, are revealing. Bill Clinton's status as the first male presidential candidate and his breaking of a historic gender barrier appear to have altered the usual gendered responses to Democratic politicians and, more importantly, Democratic candidate spouses. The lack of a traditional gender gap means that Bill Clinton generated more positive responses from men than is typical or, alternatively, that he failed to benefit from the women affinity effect, which buoyed the evaluations of Michelle Obama in both 2008 and 2012 (Burrell 2001; Elder and Frederick 2017). It is also possible that due to the scandals discussed previously his favorability among women lessened.

Figure 5.3 indicates that opinions of Melania Trump did not differ greatly among men and women either. The bivariate analysis shows that about 39 percent of men and women evaluated her favorably. Although not shown, it is notable that male respondents were six percentage points more likely than female respondents to indicate that they had no opinion of or had never heard of Melania Trump, indicating women were slightly more aware of her presence in the campaign than were men. This suggests Melania Trump broke through the awareness of women more than she did for men.

Gender is not a significant predictor of favorability toward Melania Trump in the multivariate models (Table 5.3). While Melania Trump did not have a particularly strong appeal among women, the lack of a gap between women and men once again is noteworthy as most Republican

Table 5.2 Logistic regression models predicting respondents' favorability rating toward Bill Clinton

Independent variable	*Model 1*	*Model 2*	*Model 3*
Demographic variables			
Age	−0.002* (0.006)	−0.011* (0.006)	−0.020* (0.006)
Education	0.089 (0.075)	0.163* (0.069)	0.063 (0.070)
Income	−0.042 (0.055)	−0.001 (0.051)	−0.027 (0.041)
Black	−0.483 (0.392)	0.263 (0.325)	−0.470 (0.363)
Hispanic	−0.029 (0.178)	0.000 (0.143)	−0.024 (0.157)
Female	−0.324 (0.216)	−0.112 (0.198)	−0.244 (0.204)
White Born Again Evangelical	0.012 (0.251)	−0.041 (0.236)	−0.191 (0.235)
White non-college educated	−0.900 (1.020)	−0.517 (0.894)	−0.920 (0.981)
Urban	−0.415 (0.255)	−0.336 (0.232)	−0.270 (0.238)
Rural	−001 (0.265)	−0.055 (0.248)	−0.104 (0.254)
Political variables			
Partisanship (more Republican)	−0.500* (0.094)	−0.850* (0.078)	
Ideology (more liberal)	0.248 (0.129)	0.386* (0.112)	
Melania Trump favorability	0.025 (0.253)	−0.262 (0.213)	−0.009 (0.222)
Donald Trump favorability	−0.225 (0.289)		−0.968* (0.229)
Hillary Clinton favorability	2.358* (0.290)		3.152* (0.233)
Constant	1.201 (0.763)	1.732* (0.707)	0.485 (0.457)
Pseudo R^2	0.596	0.519	0.561
N	769	769	769

Notes: Dependent variable is 1 coded for respondents rating Bill Clinton favorable and 0 otherwise. Standard errors in parentheses

*$p < 0.05$

political figures fare significantly worse among women. Donald Trump's evaluations, for example, suffered from a significant gender gap with women less likely to view him favorably than men; however, gender was basically a non-factor in predicting support for Melania Trump. In this sense then, Melania Trump stands apart from other prominent Republican political figures and stands with her predecessor Ann Romney. Similar to Ann Romney, Melania Trump was not particularly effective at appealing to women, but neither did she provoke a distinctively negative response from women as her husband and other Republican presidential candidates have done.

Race and Ethnicity

The 2016 presidential election was notable as the first election since 2004 without an African American presidential candidate spouse and candidate. Michelle Obama's departure from the political scene as the first African

Table 5.3 Logistic regression models predicting respondents' favorability rating toward Melania Trump

Independent variable	*Model 1*	*Model 2*	*Model 3*
Demographic variables			
Age	0.019* (0.006)	0.019* (0.005)	0.019* (0.005)
Education	0.145* (0.067)	0.048 (0.060)	0.171* (0.065)
Income	0.102* (0.048)	0.113* (0.045)	0.123* (0.047)
Black	−0.062 (0.372)	−0.372 (0.344)	0.100 (0.365)
Hispanic	−0.031 (0.158)	−0.037 (0.040)	−0.152 (0.135)
Female	0.018 (0.186)	0.097 (0.172)	0.052 (0.182)
White Born Again Evangelical	−0.298 (0.219)	−0.116 (0.201)	−0.205 (0.212)
White non-college educated	0.873 (0.904)	1.011 (0.822)	1.055 (0.877)
Urban	0.219 (0.220)	0.254 (0.203)	0.151 (0.214)
Rural	0.499* (0.232)	0.379 (0.214)	0.429 (0.227)
Political variables			
Partisanship (more Republican)	0.139 (0.093)	0.496* (0.074)	
Ideology (more liberal)	−0.121 (0.115)	−0.261* (0.106)	
Bill Clinton favorability	0.077 (0.301)	−0.234 (0.214)	
Donald Trump favorability	2.093* (0.239)		2.302* (0.219)
Hillary Clinton favorability	−0.474 (0.301)		−0.775* (0.268)
Constant	−3.605* (0.760)	−2.866* (0.690)	−3.752 (0.546)
Pseudo R^2	0.428	0.314	0.426
N	769	769	769

Notes: Dependent variable is 1 coded for respondents rating Bill Clinton favorable and 0 otherwise. Standard errors in parentheses

$^*p < 0.05$

American first lady had the potential to lessen the role of race in the public's evaluation of 2016 presidential candidate spouses. Yet, voting in the 2016 presidential election broke down heavily along racial lines (Abramowitz 2017; Sabato 2017). Part of this divide can be attributed to long-term partisan attachments among various groups of voters. However, Donald Trump's history of questioning of the birth place of President Barack Obama and his inflammatory remarks about Mexican immigrants in his campaign announcement speech generated highly negative reactions among people of color (Baretto et al. 2017).

African Americans were particularly favorable in their evaluations of Michelle Obama in both 2008 and 2012, even after controlling for partisan attachments and other potentially confounding variables. The question here is whether Bill Clinton would retain this strong affinity in 2016. Bill Clinton, similar to most Democratic political leaders, enjoys high levels of support from African American and Hispanic voters, and this support was crucial in Hillary Clinton's winning coalition during the Democratic presidential primary against Senator Bernie Sanders. The analyses presented here, however, suggest that African Americans' distinctive warmth was specific to Michelle Obama and did not extend to her successor. While Bill Clinton enjoyed high favorable ratings among African Americans (Fig. 5.3), neither race nor ethnicity was a significant predictor in the multivariate models (Table 5.2). Similar to the role of gender, this lack of effect speaks to the role of symbolic representation in driving evaluation of candidate spouses. It appears that African Americans felt warmly toward Michelle Obama over and above their heavily Democratic partisanship because she descriptively represented them. Without the presence of a Black candidate spouse, this effect dissipated in 2016. And despite his efforts to target rural White voters, Bill Clinton's evaluations were not distinctively more favorable among any of these groups either.

Similar to prior Republican candidate spouses (and most Republican political figures), Melania Trump had low favorable ratings among African Americans and Hispanics (Fig. 5.3); yet neither race nor ethnicity predicted a less favorable opinion of her in the multivariate models (Table 5.3). Thus, African Americans and Hispanics did not view her in a particular negative light all else considered. Nor did Melania Trump benefit from particularly favorable reactions from White voters including White working class voters and evangelicals, groups who supported her husband in very high numbers (Sabato 2017).

Age

Recent US presidential elections have seen a generational divide in voting patterns and political attitudes. Younger people, also referred to as the millennial generation, have drifted toward much more Democratic views in their partisan leanings and candidate choices in recent years (Sides and Vavreck 2013). Individual-level analysis shows that the generational divide that has emerged in the US politics remains alive and well even when evaluating the spouses of presidential candidates. Bill Clinton was viewed most positively among young voters and had the lowest favorable ratings among older voters.[5] Age is in fact the only statistically significant demographic predictor across all three models of the multivariate models predicting favorability for Bill Clinton ($p < 0.05$). These results are consistent with the idea that young voters are more comfortable relative to older voters with a male candidate spouse and with a spouse who many believed would play an active policy role in the White House. The pattern is reversed for Melania Trump. Melania Trump is rated more favorably among older Americans and not well liked by younger Americans ($p < 0.05$). These results are consistent with the idea that young Americans view Melania Trump less favorably not only because they are less Republican in general but because they resonate more with candidate spouses showcasing their own autonomy rather than playing a traditionally behind-the-scenes role.[6]

Political Variables

Given the ideological and partisan polarization of American politics as well as the historic unpopularity of the 2016 presidential candidates, it is also important to assess the role that partisanship, ideology, and views toward the candidates themselves had on public evaluations of Bill Clinton and Melania Trump.

Partisanship stands out as a strong indicator of support for both candidate spouses in 2016, although considerably less so for Melania Trump than for Bill Clinton. For Bill Clinton, 82 percent of Democrats and only 23 percent of Republicans viewed him favorably (Fig. 5.3). With a 58 percentage point difference in support between Democrats and Republicans, Bill Clinton had the widest partisan gap in favorability of any modern presidential spouse. The fact that 72 percent of Republicans viewed Bill Clinton unfavorably is consistent with the theory of negative partisanship developed in earlier chapters and also fairly typical for nationally known Democratic political figures.

The multivariate models (Table 5.2) show that despite being strongly correlated with support for the presidential candidates, partisanship exerted a negative and statistically significant impact on feelings toward Bill Clinton in the two models for which it was included ($p < 0.05$), indicating that Republicans evaluated him negatively and Democrats evaluated him positively. This is not surprising considering he has been a figure on the US political scene for more than two decades. Analyzing the results in model 2 in Table 5.2 shows that controlling for all other variables, the marginal effect of moving from the strongest Republicans to the strongest Democrats on the five-point partisanship scale increased the likelihood of expressing a favorable view toward Bill Clinton by 74 percentage points. Examining the relationship to ideology shows that liberals were more favorable toward Clinton than conservatives, but this relationship was only statistically significant in the models excluding the presidential candidates.

Party polarization and negative partisanship were notably less pronounced in evaluations of Melania Trump. As shown in Fig. 5.3, 64 percent of Republicans and 21 percent of Democrats viewed her favorably, resulting in a 43 percent partisan gap. While this is a sizable gap, it is smaller than the partisan gap in response to Bill Clinton as well as other modern candidate spouses. Additionally, reactions of the opposition party loyalists to Melania Trump were less hostile than those toward Bill Clinton, as only 54 percent of Democrats expressed an unfavorable view of her (as compared to 72 percent for Bill Clinton).

In the models predicting favorability of Melania Trump, partisanship and ideology were only statistically significant in the model excluding assessments of Donald Trump and Hillary Clinton ($p < 0.05$). As expected, Republicans were more favorable toward Melania Trump than Democrats. Analyzing the results in model 2 shows that controlling for all other variables in the model, the marginal effect of moving from the strongest Democrats to the strongest Republicans on the five-point partisanship scale led to an increased likelihood of expressing a favorable view toward Melania Trump by 51 percentage points. Once again, this is considerably less than the margin effects of partisanship on views of Bill Clinton as discussed above.

The results concerning partisanship support two important points. First, evaluations of the candidate spouses are highly partisan. Despite the efforts of candidate spouses to rise above the partisan fray or to remove themselves completely from the partisan fray, as Melania Trump did throughout much of the 2016 campaign, both candidate spouses were undeniably viewed through partisan lenses. Partisan polarization was a major factor in shaping public perceptions toward them and acted to constrain the popularity of these figures.

The results also reveal that public evaluations of Bill Clinton were more polarized along partisan lines than those of Melania Trump. This finding makes sense given Bill Clinton's high-profile and lengthy political career. Melania Trump is quite simply a less political figure—she was new to the political scene and she chose to play a minor role in the campaign—and as a result, her evaluations are less partisan. What this also means, however, is that Melania Trump's historically low favorable ratings are not the product of ever-increasing or unprecedented partisan polarization. Indeed, public reactions toward her are less polarized along party lines than any spouse since Laura Bush in 2004. Rather than Melania Trump acting as a blank slate for the projection of contemporary partisan polarization, her low approval ratings are the result of both Republicans and Democrats viewing her less favorably compared to her predecessors. Thus, other factors beyond partisanship must account for her distinctively low favorable ratings.

Evaluations of Presidential Candidates

In keeping with the findings presented in previous chapters, the most pronounced factor in shaping opinions toward the 2016 major party presidential candidate spouses was in fact public opinion toward their spouses, the presidential candidates. Of those individuals with a favorable view of Donald Trump, 72 percent rated Melania Trump favorably (Fig. 5.3). And of those individuals with a favorable view of Hillary Clinton, 88 percent rated Bill Clinton favorably.

Turning to the multivariate models, the strongest predictor of support for Melania Trump in 2016 was support for Donald Trump ($p < 0.05$). Excluding partisanship and ideology from the model, the marginal effect of a favorable response toward Donald Trump increased the likelihood of support for Melania Trump by 50 percentage points.

Similarly, citizens who felt positively toward Hillary Clinton were more likely to feel that way about Bill Clinton, while individuals who felt favorable toward Donald Trump were less favorable to Bill Clinton ($p < 0.05$). Excluding partisanship and ideology from the model, the marginal effect of a favorable response toward Hillary Clinton increased the likelihood of support for Bill Clinton by 61 percentage points.

Taken together, these results reveal that evaluations of both candidate spouses were heavily shaped by evaluations of the candidates; however, in both the bivariate analysis and the multivariate analysis, the substantive impact of this relationship was stronger for the Clintons than for the Trumps. This result is surprising for a couple of reasons. Given that Bill Clinton was an elected figure in his own right, one might anticipate greater divergence in the way the public perceived him and his wife, than in the case of the Trumps. Also, one possible explanation for Melania Trump's historically low approval ratings offered earlier in the chapter was that perceptions of her were defined more strongly than usual by perceptions of her unpopular husband due to her low-profile role on the campaign trail. Yet, this was not the case. Perceptions of Donald Trump, while a very important factor shaping perceptions of Melania Trump, were a weaker force in shaping perceptions of her than in the case of other candidate spouses, including Bill Clinton. Thus, evaluations of Donald Trump, similar to the effects of negative partisanship, certainly acted as a drag on Melania Trump's favorable ratings; however, they alone cannot explain her status as the least popular candidate spouse in the modern era.

The results also show that while candidate evaluations are a strong force shaping perceptions of their spouses, they are not determinative. For instance, 26 percent of individuals with an unfavorable view of Hillary Clinton rated Bill Clinton favorably. Among individuals viewing Donald Trump unfavorably, 13 percent approved of Melania Trump (Fig. 5.3). These numbers show that there is some degree of independence in spousal evaluations. This independence is likely driven by the feeling among a significant minority of Americans that presidential candidate spouses should be viewed with more sympathy than other people campaigning on behalf of presidential candidates (Gfk Omni survey 2017). This in turn helps explain why even though Melania Trump and Bill Clinton were unpopular compared to previous candidate spouses, they were still more popular than their spouses, Hillary Clinton and Donald Trump.

As discussed in the previous two chapters, favorable views of candidate spouses acted as predictors of feelings toward the other spouse. In other words, positive feelings toward Ann Romney predicted positive feelings toward Michelle Obama and vice versa. The same pattern characterized views of Hillary Clinton and Barbara Bush. The multivariate analyses predicting each spouse's favorability rating in 2016, however, show that Melania Trump was not a significant predictor of favorability toward Bill Clinton in any of the three models, nor did attitudes toward Bill Clinton have discernable effects on perceptions of Melania Trump. This break from the past underscores, once again, how unusual the 2016 presidential candidate spouses were in the eye of the public.

Discussion and Conclusion

Americans have long preferred traditional presidential candidate spouses—those that signal they have no interest in shaping policy or exerting political influence. They now also expect candidate spouses to be visible and active on the campaign trail, expectations reinforced by well-received performances of Michelle Obama and Ann Romney in 2012. For a variety of reasons neither Bill Clinton nor Melania Trump fulfilled the new traditional expectations for candidate spouses, and, as a result, they are the two least well-liked candidate spouses over the past three decades. The intense partisanship characterizing the 2016 campaign environment and the historic unpopularity of their spouses also played a role in diminishing the popularity of the 2016 candidate spouses in the eyes of Americans.

This chapter argues that Melania Trump fulfilled neither set of new traditional expectations for candidate spouses. While Melania Trump was supportive of her husband, effectively signaled her dedication to motherhood, and was clearly removed from political or policy influence, her image was nevertheless not traditional. In addition to being an immigrant, which defied the traditional image of American presidential candidate spouses (Mandziuk 2017) and might have limited her engagement in the public political realm, Melania Trump was engulfed in several scandals across the 2016 campaign revolving around nude photos, plagiarism, and potential violations of immigration laws, which made her a more complicated and controversial figure than the traditional candidate spouse. Her favorability ratings were further weighed down by the record-setting unpopularity of Donald Trump, which made it an enormous challenge to appeal to the American public no matter how she positioned herself during the campaign, but adopting a relatively low profile made it much more difficult for to rise above her husband's poor ratings.

The new traditionalism expectations were also significantly challenged by Melania Trump's near invisibility on the campaign trail. While Donald Trump won the presidency without his wife's active presence on the campaign trail, her absence marks a striking departure from the role of modern presidential candidate spouses. Melania Trump's decision to not be a major surrogate for her husband may create more opportunities for future presidential candidate spouses to opt out of the relentless campaign duties and schedules typical of modern spouses. However, it also appears to have contributed to her low popularity. Because she was not active on the campaign trail, creating opportunities for positive coverage, Melania Trump may have been more vulnerable to being defined by the negative news stories that emerged, such as her history of working without legal documentation and her partially plagiarized convention speech. While partisan polarization and negative views of her husband certainly hurt Melania Trump's favorability in the eyes of Americans, these forces were not as determinative for her approval ratings as they are for many other contemporary spouses including Bill Clinton, Michelle Obama, and Ann Romney. Once again, rather than her low-profile campaign role allowing her to be defined by her husband, it seems that her decision to defy Americans' desire to get to know the individuals vying to become first spouse drove her low ratings.

Bill Clinton was in many ways a dramatic contrast to Melania Trump. Rather than being defined by 2016 campaign coverage, Bill Clinton entered the 2016 campaign with almost universal name recognition. As an ex-president, he was better known than any non-incumbent spouse in modern history. Many voters already possessed concrete opinions of him based on partisanship, ideology, and his public and private conduct as president. While Bill Clinton enjoyed more positive evaluations than his spouse overall, his ratings were highly polarized along partisan lines. Republicans were especially more willing to express negative views of him than the opposing party identifiers were of spouses in the past.

Moreover, Bill Clinton became slightly less popular as the campaign unfolded, as his record as president actually became a liability in Hillary Clinton's primary campaign against Senator Bernie Sanders and his personal history with women and the Clinton Foundation became consistent attack lines from the Trump campaign in the general election. Despite his relatively poor image, Bill Clinton did not suffer the steep decline in favorability ratings to the same extent that Hillary Clinton experienced. Although the sample size is very limited, this shows that even candidate spouses with an extensive political resume enjoy a reservoir of good will that inflates their political support above the level of the presidential candidate.

While Bill Clinton took on some of the typical responsibilities of the modern candidate spouse such as being a major surrogate on the campaign trail and drawing on his intimate knowledge of his spouse as a wife and mother to explain why she would make a great president, he also does not fit the idea of a "new traditional" first spouse and certainly not the image of "old traditional" presidential spouse. Given his unique career of having been president as well as a policy agenda of his own and political history including high-profile scandals, it could hardly be otherwise. In promoting Hillary Clinton's policies, his policy record would always be part of the story. Given his experience, few would expect him not to have a policy advisory role in a Hillary Clinton White House. One would hardly expect him to choose a non-controversial policy platform such as literacy, mental health, or childhood obesity to promote the type of activities Americans find the most acceptable for presidential spouses. His status as a former president, as someone interested in shaping policy in his wife's administration, and his status as the first-ever male candidate spouse made him far from typical or traditional. This was reflected in both the amount and nature of pollster inquiries about him during the election. The unique nature of Bill Clinton's political experience makes evaluating the extent to which gender influenced public evaluations of him a more difficult challenge. Would the public express more favorable attitudes to a male spouse who did not seek to play as prominent a role in his wife's administration? The answer would likely be "yes," but there cannot be a more definitive answer until another male is in that position in the future.

Notes

1. YouGov/*The Economist* conducted poll during July 23–24, 2016. The sample included 1300 general population respondents with a margin of error of ±4.2 percent (4.5 percent for registered voters).
2. Questions specifically about Bill Clinton historical role as former president were not included, for example, polls asking respondents to rank who is the best president of all time. Only questions regarding Bill Clinton's role in the campaign or relationship to his presidential candidate spouse were included.
3. This poll was conducted for CNN by ORC International, October 20–22, 2016, and based on 1017 telephone interviews. The sample consisted of national adults. It included 517 interviews of landline respondents and 500 interviews of cell phone respondents.
4. This strategy employed by the Clinton campaign was in part driven by the urban-rural divide in the 2016 election. Bill Clinton's roots in rural Arkansas led the campaign to give him a lead role in appealing to this demographic. Nevertheless, the Democratic Party has historically fared well among urban dwellers, while the Republicans have been the top choice among rural voters in most elections, and this urban-rural divide has become heightened in recent years (McKee 2008). The presidential election of 2016 was no exception as Hillary Clinton crushed Donald Trump among urbanites, while he trounced her with individuals living in rural areas (Scala and Johnson 2017). On the basis of this evidence, we expect a similar urban-rural divide in evaluations of the presidential candidate spouses, with Melania Trump viewed more favorably among rural citizens and Bill Clinton more popular among individuals in urban areas. These relationships are reported in the demographic sections of both the bivariate and multivariate analyses.
5. While still very strong, Bill Clinton's favorability rating among the youngest demographic was actually depressed by the fact that 23.5 percent had never heard of or had no opinion of Bill Clinton. A reminder that many of them were too young to have personal recollections of his presidency.
6. According to the Gfk Omni survey (2017), a majority of young Americans feel it is appropriate for candidate spouses to speak about their own accomplishments on the campaign trail, whereas a majority of older Americans feel this is inappropriate.

Bibliography

Abramowitz, Alan I. 2017. It Wasn't the Economy Stupid, White Racial Resentment, and the Rise of Trump. In *Trumped: The Election that Broke All of the Rules*, ed. Larry J. Sabato, Kyle Kondik, and Geoffrey Skelly, 202–210. Lanham, MD: Rowman and Littlefield.

Baretto, Matt, Thomas Schaller, and Gary Segura. 2017. Latinos and the 2016 Election. In *Trumped: The Election that Broke All of the Rules*, ed. Larry J. Sabato, Kyle Kondik, and Geoffrey Skelly, 123–135. Lanham, MD: Rowman and Littlefield.

Berenson, Tessa. 2016. Hillary Clinton Struggles to Defend 1994 Crime Bill. April 15. http://time.com/4295463/hillary-clinton-struggles-to-defend-1994-crime-bill/

Borrelli, MaryAnne. 2011. *The Politics of the President's Wife*. College Station, TX: Texas A&M University Press.

Burrell, Barbara. 2001. *Public Opinion, the First Ladyship, and Hillary Rodham Clinton*. New York: Routledge.

Caldwell, Alicia A, Chad Day, and Jake Pearson. 2016. Melania Trump Modeled in US Prior to Getting Work Visa. *Associated Press*, November 5.

Caroli, Betty Boyd. 2010. *First Ladies: From Martha Washington to Michelle Obama*. Oxford: Oxford University Press.

Chozick, Amy. 2016. Hillary Clinton Shapes Potential New Role for Bill Clinton. *The New York Times*, May 16.

Dittmar, Kelly. 2012. Turning the Tables: Behind Every Successful Woman. In *Women and Executive Office: Pathways and Performance*, ed. Melody Rose, 231–258. Lynne Rienner Publishers.

———. 2015. Gender Expectations and the Presidential Partnership. Center for American Women and Politics, Presidential Gender Watch. http://presidentialgenderwatch.org/gender-expectations-and-the-presidential-partnership/

Duerst-Lahti, Georgia. 2014. Presidential Elections: Gendered Space and the Case of 2012. In *Gender and Elections: Shaping the Future of American Politics*, ed. Susan J. Carroll and Richard L. Fox, 3rd ed., 16–48. Cambridge: Cambridge University Press.

Elder, Laurel, and Brian Frederick. 2017. Perceptions of Candidate Spouses in the 2012 Presidential Election: The Role of Gender, Race, Religion, and Partisanship. *Politics, Groups, and Identities*. https://doi.org/10.1080/21565503.2017.1338969.

Fuller, Jaime. 2015. First Man? First Dude? 'Adam?' The TBD Title of the First Male White House Spouse. *Washington Post*, January 25, 2015.

Gfk Omni Survey. 2017. KnowledgePanel (KP) OmniWeb Survey Conducted by Gfk Custom Research LLC, September 15–17.

Haberman, Maggie, and Michael Barbaro. 2016. How Melania Trump's Speech Veered Off Course and Caused an Uproar. *The New York Times*, July 19.

Horowitz, Jason. 2016. Bill Clinton Evokes Past, but From Periphery of Wife's Campaign. *New York Times*, November 6, 2016.

Ioffe, Julia. 2016. Melania Trump on Her Rise, Her Family Secrets, and Her True Political Views: 'Nobody Will Ever Know'. *GQ Magazine*, April 27.

Jordan, Mary, and Stephanie McCrummen. 2016. After Convention Stumble Melania Trump has Largely Stumbled From Campaign Trail. *Washington Post*, September 8, 2016.

Karni, Annie. 2016. Can Bill Clinton Win Back the Bubba Vote? *Politico*, July 26.

MacManus, Susan A., and Andrew F. Quecan. 2008. Spouses as Campaign Surrogates: Strategic Appearances by Presidential and Vice Presidential Candidates' Wives in the 2004 Election. *PS, Political Science & Politics* 42 (2): 337–348.

Mandziuk, Roseann M. 2017. Whither the Good Wife? 2016 Presidential Candidate Spouses in the Gendered Spaces of Contemporary Politics. *Quarterly Journal of Speech* 103 (1–2): 136–159.

McKee, Seth. 2008. Rural Voters and the Polarization of American Presidential Elections. *PS: Political Science and Politics* 41 (1): 101–108.

Merica, Dan. 2015. Bill Clinton on 2016: 'My Role Should Primarily Be as a Backstage Adviser'. *CNNpolitics.com*, April 7. Accessed July 20, 2015. http://www.cnn.com/2015/04/07/politics/bill-clinton-2016-role

Parker, Ashley. 2016. Donald Trump, Stumbling with Women, Enlists Wife to Campaign. *The New York Times*, April 4.

Rappeport, Alan. 2016. Melania Trump, Solo in Pennsylvania, Tries to Smooth Husband's Rough Edges. *The New York Times*, November 3.

Reinhart, R.J. 2017. Ivanka Trump Gets Less Negative Ratings than Her Father. *Gallup*, May 17.

Saad, Lydia. 2016. Melania Trump's Image Less Positive than Other Spouses. *Gallup*, July 18.

Sabato, Larry J. 2017. The Election that Broke All or At Least Most of the Rules. In *Trumped: The Election that Broke All of the Rules*, ed. Larry J. Sabato, Kyle Kondik, and Geoffrey Skelly, 1–29. Lanham, MD: Rowman and Littlefield.

Scala, Dante J., and Kenneth M. Johnson. 2017. Political Polarization along the Rural-Urban Continuum? The Geography of the Presidential Vote, 2000–2016. *The Annals of the American Academy of Political and Social Science* 672 (1): 162–184.

Schreckinger, Ben, and Gabriel Debenedetti. 2016. Gaps in Melania Trump's Immigration Story Raise Questions. *Politico*, August 4.

Sides, John, and Lynn Vavreck. 2013. *The Gamble: Choice and Chance in the 2012 Presidential Election*. Princeton, NJ: Princeton University Press.

Stack, Liam. 2016. Donald Trump Featured Paula Jones and 2 Other Women Who Accused Bill Clinton of Sexual Assault. *New York Times*, October 9.

Talbot, Margaret. 2016. What Bill Clinton Should Do as First Gentleman. *The New Yorker*, November 2.

Thurman, Judith. 2004. The Candidate's Wife: Teresa Heinz Kerry is an Uncharted Element on the Road to the White House. *The New Yorker*, September 27.

Trebay, Guy. 2015. Melania Trump, the Silent Partner. *The New York Times*, September 30.

Wright, Lauren. 2016. *On Behalf of the President: Presidential Spouses and White House Communications Strategy Today*. Praeger.

———. 2017. Melania Trump Refuses to Act Like a First Lady. Good for Her. *Washington Post*, January 19.

YouGov/*The Economist* Poll. 2016. July 23–24, 2016. https://today.yougov.com/news/2016/07/25/yougoveconomist-poll-july-23-24-2016/

CHAPTER 6

The Future of Public Opinion and Presidential Candidate Spouses

This concluding chapter revisits the broad theoretical frameworks that guide the analyses of public opinion toward presidential candidate spouses throughout the book: new traditionalism, conditional incumbency advantage, symbolic representation, the impact of party polarization, and the degree to which evaluations of candidate spouses are both dependent on and independent of evaluations of the candidates themselves. This chapter considers what both the trend data analyzed in Chap. 2 and the in-depth examinations of six candidate spouses during three presidential elections, 1992, 2012, and 2016, tell us about public perceptions of presidential candidate spouses. This chapter considers the meaning of the collective findings for the future role of candidate spouses in presidential elections, for the role of first ladies and possible first gentlemen, and for understanding gender equality and the role of women in society and politics more broadly. This chapter concludes by building on the foundation established to highlight opportunities for further research on how the public views presidential candidate spouses and the spouses of other major political figures running for office.

Presidential Candidate Spouses and New Traditionalism

The role of candidate spouses in presidential campaigns has changed dramatically since 1988, the year that the empirical analyses in this book begin. The political landscape Kitty Dukakis and Barbara Bush confronted

L. Elder et al., *American Presidential Candidate Spouses*,
https://doi.org/10.1007/978-3-319-73879-6_6

in the 1988 presidential election was far different from what Melania Trump and Bill Clinton had to deal with during the 2016 campaign. Media scrutiny of presidential candidate spouses has become much more intense and has spread across multiple platforms, including the complicated and often combative world of social media. The spouses of presidential candidates cannot avoid the harsh media spotlight, even if that is what they desire, as appeared to be the case with Melania Trump during the 2016 presidential campaign. This high level of media attention sparks the interest of voters and puts the candidates' spouses under the microscope of the public's gaze. Presidential candidate spouses typically become objects of fascination even among those who are not interested in political news more generally.

The public has developed lofty expectations for presidential candidate spouses. While the spouses of presidential candidates have a long history of helping their husbands' campaigns, starting in 1992, candidate spouses began to play a markedly more prominent and more visible role in campaigns, leading to a new, higher level of expectations for the individuals performing this role. As the 2017 survey data collected for this book make clear, Americans want the opportunity to learn about the candidates' spouses and think it is important to see them campaigning on behalf of their spouse (Gfk Omni survey 2017). There is a sense among the public that it is through the actions and statements of the candidates' spouses that they can better understand the genuine character and essence of the presidential candidates. Lauren Wright (2016a) has found that the unique personal knowledge of the candidate that spouses can offer makes them a most effective campaign surrogate.

The role of the modern presidential candidate spouse is precariously balanced between the private and public spheres. Presidential candidate spouses are thrust into the public spotlight not because they are personally interested in seeking a public platform or political power, but on the basis of a very private act, whom they chose to marry. Despite the private nature of their connection to the candidate, they are now expected to play a highly public role in contemporary presidential elections.

At the same time that expectations for candidate spouses to act as public figures have grown, what the public wants from presidential candidate spouses in terms of the nature of their actions has remained decidedly traditional as evidenced by the fact that 46 percent of Americans do not think it is appropriate for presidential candidate spouses to highlight their own accomplishments on the campaign trail (Gfk Omni survey 2017).

Even in the twenty-first century, most Americans do not want presidential spouses to play a role shaping decisions or policy in the president's administration.

Navigating the somewhat conflicting expectations of new traditionalism—the expectation to be a highly visible campaign surrogate but within the context of a traditionally supportive role—is a major challenge for anyone who becomes a presidential candidate spouse. The empirical evidence presented in this book confirms that the spouses successfully striking the ideal balance between being a visible campaign surrogate and embodying a traditional and supportive role enjoy strong favorable ratings. This balance is revealed in the cases of incumbent spouses Barbara Bush and Michelle Obama, as well as the first-time presidential candidate spouse Ann Romney in 2012. All three of these women carefully navigated the expectations of new traditionalism and were rewarded with favorable reviews from the public.

Those spouses who depart from the new traditional expectations in some meaningful way—by remaining near invisible on the campaign trail as was the case with Melania Trump in 2016 or by signaling an intention to influence policy and decision-making as was the case with Hillary Clinton in 1992 and Bill Clinton in 2016—suffer from lower levels of public support. Chapter 1 posed the argument that one of the primary reasons to study candidate spouses is that they are highly visible, effective political actors. Melania Trump's decision to stay away from the campaign trail for the majority of the 2016 election season is contrary to this very basic idea, and defied public expectations (Gfk Omni Survey 2017). This decision in turn helps explain why she was the least popular candidate spouse in modern times.

New Traditionalism and Implications for Incumbent First Ladies

This book also advances the argument that the concept of incumbency advantage, typically applied to elected officials (Ansolabehere and Snyder 2004; Jacobson and Carson 2015; Mayhew 2008) also applies to presidential spouses, although the benefits of incumbency for presidential spouses are conditional. Incumbent first ladies have the opportunity to utilize the stature, resources, and responsibilities of the Office of the First Lady to increase their visibility and strengthen their approval ratings among the public, much like incumbent members of Congress.

Importantly, incumbent presidential spouses also have the opportunity to demonstrate in a concrete way that they do in fact comport with the public's expectations about how the first spouse should conduct herself/himself.

The analyses presented in this book indicate that incumbent spouses that comport themselves within the expectations of new traditionalism—as illustrated in the cases of Barbara Bush and Michelle Obama—benefit from a meaningful boost in their public approval from their first to second election season. In contrast, first spouses that defy traditional expectations, as Hillary Clinton did through her leadership of the health care task force, end up losing favorability among the public. Thus, the expectations of new traditionalism not only shape public evaluations of candidate spouses when they first enter the national scene as campaign surrogates, but also condition whether a presidential spouse is able to increase her or his popularity while inhabiting the White House.

In January 2017, Melania Trump assumed the position of first lady under the long shadow of Michelle Obama, who in many ways perfected and reinforced the ideal balancing act of new traditionalism. Michelle Obama set a standard in this regard that is a tough act for anyone to follow, much less someone with the limited political background of Melania Trump. Whether Melania Trump will benefit from an incumbency advantage going into the 2020 election is an open question. During her brief time on the national political scene, she has both challenged and conformed to the expectations of new traditionalism.

Much as she did during the 2016 presidential campaign, after becoming first lady, Melania Trump shied from the public role Americans have come to expect for presidential spouses. Most prominently, she decided not to move into the White House until the summer of 2017 after their son finished his school year (Cilliza 2017). Soon after Barack Obama was elected president in 2008, the news media were running stories about the first family's transition to Washington, DC. Pollsters asked the public questions concerning the Obama's decision to put their daughters in school in the Washington DC area as well as multiple questions about the kind of puppy the Obamas should get, underscoring Americans' fascination with the first family. Melania Trump's decision to remain in New York City with their son for the first six months of her husband's presidency made these kinds of feel-good White House family stories harder to write. On the contrary, news reports explored the impact of her decision to remain in New York City in terms of the costs to taxpayers for the additional secret service required and on how Donald Trump's lack of family in the White House might be affecting his perspective and decision-making as president (Fandos 2017; Thrush and Haberman 2017).

Since becoming first lady, Melania Trump has given far fewer speeches than previous first ladies (Goodin 2017). Her first major public appearance as first lady was not until March 29, 2017, when she made a short speech at the International Women of Courage ceremony at the State Department (Puente 2017). In contrast to Michelle Obama's high-profile work championing a number of feel-good causes throughout her first term as first lady—including the organic White House garden, the Let's Move campaign promoting children's health, and work on behalf of military families—Melania Trump has assumed a much lower profile and less public role. As of mid-August 2017, she had yet to formally identify a cause she would champion (Goodin 2017).

One example of her voicing her opinion on an issue—the serious problem of childhood bullying—drew mixed opinions from political observers. Most of the criticism centered not on the substance of the issue but on whether she was an appropriate messenger to promote this topic in light of President Donald Trump's string of controversial comments attacking various individuals and segments of the population. As *The Washington Post* noted, Melania Trump's "mention of bullying was immediately complicated because of her husband's bellicose approach to public life" (Thompson 2017). Media reporting suggests this possible initiative has now been placed on the back burner (Goodin 2017). Nevertheless, the reaction to Melania Trump's comments on this issue is a stark reminder that even when she tries to speak out on seemingly non-controversial subjects, an activity the public almost unanimously supports the first lady doing as revealed in Chap. 2, she may face difficulties. The polarizing and overpowering nature of Donald Trump's political profile may pose unique challenges for Melania Trump as she tries to carve out a distinct political cause, challenges with which no other presidential spouses have had to contend.

Thus, not only did Melania Trump defy public expectations by staying away from the campaign trail for the majority of the election, but she is also defying expectations regarding the public role of first ladies. Perhaps because she has said so little, one of the most prominent themes in news coverage of First Lady Melania Trump has been fashion including close attention to her clothing choices on her trips abroad; however, even her fashion coverage has been fraught with some controversy, as there was much media criticism of her wearing high heels on a visit to Texas to survey damage in the aftermath of Hurricane Harvey.

On the other hand, other aspects of her performance as first lady have been fairly traditional. In fact, Melania Trump has repeatedly indicated she would like to be a traditional first lady (Goodin 2017). She has maintained a focus on her son and has presented herself as a silent supportive partner to her husband. And although she has not specifically adopted a cause as of this writing, she has made numerous visits to hospitals where she spends time with children, and her spokesperson indicated that Melania Trump's efforts as first lady will be "focused on the health and well-being of children" (Goodin 2017), a set of issues viewed as very appropriate for first ladies, as discussed in Chap. 2. Melania Trump is also taking on some of the ceremonial roles and responsibilities of first lady including acting as hostess to the spouses of visiting foreign leaders and cohosting social events including the White House Easter Egg Roll (Puente 2017).

The concept of new traditionalism developed in this book suggests that while Melania's low-profile approach to being a presidential spouse will constrain her approval ratings, the traditional aspects of her performance will be well received. And indeed, Melania Trump's approval ratings so far are consistent with this idea. While her favorable ratings remain significantly below what Michelle Obama's were at this stage of her first term as first lady—in part because of the unusually negative drag of her husband's poor ratings, as discussed more below, and in part because she is choosing to play a much lower profile role—Melania Trump's approval ratings have increased, and she now has a net positive rating as opposed to the net negative ratings she had throughout most of the 2016 campaign (Cilliza 2017). If she continues to avoid major controversies and maintains a traditional approach to her role as first lady, it is likely she will go into the 2020 elections with higher ratings than she had in 2016. Thus, while Melania Trump may very well end up benefiting from some level of incumbency boost, it is also important to remember she begins from the lowest approval ratings of any candidate spouse in modern history.

Future of New Traditionalism

The analysis of public opinion toward presidential candidate spouses presented in this book offers a unique lens into the American public's evolving ideas about gender equality as well as the gendered expectations of the presidency and the gendered nature of power in the United States.

The new traditional expectations of presidential candidate spouses are quite clearly gendered, shaped by traditional ideas about "the good wife" being a supportive helpmate and a committed mother (Mandziuk 2017). The traditionally gendered expectations for presidential candidate spouses appear to be lagging indicators in Americans' evolving views about gender roles. Despite the tremendous changes in women's roles in American society as well as a dramatic increase in support for gender equality, Americans respond most positively to presidential candidate spouses that fit with the traditional ideals of first ladies and wives more broadly. The evidence this book has presented that presidential candidate spouses who embody these traditional roles and images are more warmly received by the American public than candidate spouses who seek autonomy as political actors by discussing their own career achievements or who explicitly seek to use the position of first spouse to influence policy, is a powerful reminder that the institution of the presidency in the US political system remains highly masculinized (Borrelli 2011; Dittmar 2015; Duerst-Lahti 2014; Mandziuk 2017; Vigil 2014). The gendered nature of the presidency not only presents a serious challenge for presidential candidate spouses, but also for women seeking this office.

Given the patterns of public opinion revealed in this book, the decision of many presidential candidate spouses to embody new traditionalism makes strategic sense. Candidate spouses can best help their spouses win the election if they themselves are popular (Burrell, Elder and Frederick 2011b). Yet, by embodying rather than challenging traditional expectations, they reinforce them. Moreover, by behaving in line with traditional expectations, candidate spouses pass up the opportunity to act as role models for gender equality. As communications scholar Tammy Vigil (2014) has noted, the traditional rhetoric and traditional issue selection of presidential candidate spouses may help their popularity, but at the cost of reinforcing the idea that political issues divide into a traditional masculine-feminine dichotomy.

Since the presidency has been the exclusive domain of male office holders, the position of candidate spouse has often provided a place for women to find a voice on the national stage. Yet, spouses like Hillary Clinton wanting to use the position of first lady to advance policy goals come into conflict with a public uncomfortable with that approach from the spouses of presidential candidates (Troy 2006). If public opinion constrains the ability of candidate spouses to play an active role in the policy process or discuss issues other than non-controversial valence issues such as literacy and children's health, this has negative implications for gender equality.

Looking to the future, there are several reasons to believe that expectations for presidential candidate spouses may evolve away from new traditionalism. Multivariate analysis (not shown) of the 2017 Gfk Omni Survey data collected for this project reveal that young people are significantly more comfortable than older people with candidate spouses discussing their own accomplishments while on the campaign trail, even while other potentially confounding factors including partisanship, income, and education are controlled. Thus, as generational replacement continues, it is likely to drive more egalitarian attitudes about the appropriate role of presidential candidate spouses.

Another factor that may spark an overhaul of traditional expectations for presidential candidate spouses would be a male assuming the role of presidential spouse. As we saw in Chap. 2, Americans are more comfortable with a male presidential spouse working for pay and running for elective office compared to a female presidential spouse. In other words, Americans are more comfortable with male presidential spouses taking on autonomous roles and activities. Once a man assumes the role of presidential spouse, expectations for the role of candidate spouse may evolve in this direction. If the public does warm to the idea of a first gentleman influencing and speaking about non-gendered policy areas, this could have a lasting impact on the public's expectations for presidential candidate spouses going forward. The results of the 2016 election, however, do not allow us to move beyond speculation on this issue. Nevertheless, it may be as men assume the position of presidential spouse, Americans will become more accepting of spouses playing more autonomous and influential roles.

While there are some reasons to think public expectations may become less traditional, there are also reasons to think the "new" expectations, which are a key part of the new traditionalism framework, may also lessen or evolve. Melania Trump defied expectations for contemporary spouses by playing a low key role on the campaign trail during the 2016 presidential election. While this decision contributed to her low favorable ratings, it is possible it may have a liberalizing or loosening impact on expectations going forward. She may have created more space for future candidate spouses to opt out of the rigorous campaign schedule and not automatically have to serve as chief surrogate. Along similar lines, Melania Trump's low key role as first lady has been championed by some feminists as a good thing. Editorials in *The Washington Post* and *The New York Times* among other high-profile news outlets have questioned why Melania Trump should have to take on the unpaid role and hectic schedule of modern first ladies if it does not comport with her own personal preferences (Weiner 2017; Wright 2017). As Barbara Burrell wrote about the first lady at the dawn of the twenty-first century, "She should be allowed to choose what to do with her life." (2001, 144). Thus, while new traditionalism remains a highly useful theoretical framework for understanding public evaluations of presidential candidate spouses, there are many ways this may be challenged over the coming years and elections.

Symbolic Representation

This book also argues that presidential candidate spouses can play important roles as symbolic representatives, a role that has not previously received attention from political scientists and other scholars. Extant research exploring the concept of symbolic representation shows that a candidate's gender, race, and the intersection of gender and race can empower and mobilize voters in congressional and presidential elections (Bobo and Gilliam 1990; Dolan 2008; Mansbridge 1999; Simien 2016). This book applies the concept of symbolic representation to the study of presidential candidate spouses. The case study chapters explore how the descriptive aspects of candidate spouses can influence public evaluations toward them and find support for the idea that presidential candidate spouses can and often do offer meaningful symbolic representation, particularly to historically disadvantaged groups, who have been virtually invisible in presidential politics and elections.

Chapter 3 shows how women felt particularly warmly toward Barbara Bush, a pattern that was repeated with Michelle Obama during the 2012 election. Both Barbara Bush and Michelle Obama were one of the few high-profile women surrogates in the 1992 and 2012 campaigns. They drew on their own experiences to speak about women's lives and issues, and in return women viewed them particularly favorably. Thus, an engine behind Barbara Bush's and Michelle Obama's strong approval ratings is distinctively warm feelings from women.

Hillary Clinton's untraditional approach to the role of presidential candidate spouse set off societal controversy about feminism and the role of women in society (Troy 2006). Women as well as the public more broadly were more divided and less positive in their reaction to Hillary Clinton than to Michelle Obama and Barbara Bush. Yet, feminists in particular warmly received her. Hillary Clinton's life choices—including her decision to continue pursuing her career throughout her husband's time in elected office in Arkansas and her desire to use the position of first lady to influence major policies—sparked a national conversation about gender roles and the role of women in society. Those with feminist sympathies viewed Hillary Clinton as representing their beliefs and as a result viewed her more warmly than others in society. Those with warm feelings toward feminists also viewed both Michelle Obama and Ann Romney more warmly, suggesting that those committed to gender equality view the role of first lady as having important symbolic power for women in particular.

The most vivid illustration of a presidential candidate spouse performing symbolic representation comes from the example of Michelle Obama. Chapter 4 shows that African Americans and women viewed Michelle Obama even more warmly than others in society. Polling data *The Washington Post* collected during Michelle Obama's time as first lady underscore this connection even further. The poll results show that women, African Americans, and especially African American women felt a special connection to Michelle Obama. In this sense, presidential candidate spouses provide a voice and a symbol to groups who have been very much excluded from presidential politics.

The past 30 years have seen intriguing changes and historic firsts for presidential candidate spouses. Many of the candidate spouses over the past several decades have had high-profile careers. We have seen the first man, first African American, first Mormon, and in the case of Melania Trump the second immigrant presidential candidate spouse. An overarching question is, to what extent have these historic firsts transformed our expectations for candidate spouses, at least in terms of their backgrounds and personal characteristics?

As discussed in Chap. 2, the traditional presidential candidate spouse has been a White woman who has devoted herself to raising her family and supporting her husband's political career. This book finds that Americans' expectations for candidate spouses in terms of the career background as well as gender, and racial and religious background are not wedded to this traditional image. As long as the candidate spouse behaves in a manner consistent with new traditionalism—and that is a significant condition requiring those with careers to forgo them, for example—Americans seem ready to embrace historic firsts in terms as candidate spouses.

As discussed in Chap. 4, Americans embraced Michelle Obama very warmly despite being the first Black American to assume the role of presidential spouse during a time of racial acrimony. Certainly racial resentment, along with partisanship, constrained her favorable ratings (Elder and Frederick 2017; Knuckey and Kim 2016), but she maintained a high level of popularity throughout the 2008 and 2012 elections and her time in the national spotlight. Her decision to operate within the expectations of new traditionalism, by giving up her own career, labeling herself "mom in chief" and advocating tirelessly on behalf of her husband, was undoubtedly a factor behind these warm ratings. Similarly, although negative attitudes toward Mormons acted as a constraint on Ann Romney's ratings, she was a popular candidate spouse, widening our nation's perspective on who can be first lady. Taken together, these findings suggest that while Melania Trump's immigrant status may have factored into her low initial approval ratings as a candidate spouse and as first lady, it is something that can be surmounted.

Whether or not being the first man to run for first spouse acted to dampen Bill Clinton's approval ratings is hard to determine given his unique background and profile. Bill Clinton did not benefit from a gender affinity advantage among women, as Barbara Bush and Michelle Obama did. Nevertheless, the results suggest the central reason for his higher than usual unfavorable ratings is that he was viewed as a national political figure rather than any bias against him because of his gender. It is likely Bill Clinton's performance as a candidate spouse may open up ideas about what a candidate spouse can look like in future elections. Future male spouses, for example, may not generate quite as many news stories questioning what the nation should call a male presidential spouse or what role this person should be expected to play.

Looking to the future of electoral politics, it is an intriguing exercise to consider how Americans might react to presidential candidates with no partner, who are unmarried, or who have a same-sex partner. For instance, would members of Lesbian, Gay, Bisexual, Transgender, Queer (LGBTQ) community share a special affinity with a spouse who identified as a member of their community? Would attitudes toward LGBTQ citizens shape how Americans view an LGBTQ spouse just as attitudes toward Mormons and African Americans influenced evaluations of Ann Romney and Michelle Romney, respectively? Moving forward, the increasingly diverse composition of American society will create more opportunities to ascertain the impact presidential candidate spouses have on symbolic representation.

Impact of Partisanship and Polarization

One of the primary reasons there is value in studying public opinion toward presidential candidate spouses is because they embody an intriguing paradox in contemporary American politics. With a couple of notable exceptions, presidential candidate spouses remain highly popular figures in an increasingly polarized and negative political environment. In other words, presidential candidate spouses are anomalous figures in contemporary American politics in terms of their popularity and their relatively broad appeal. While it is the case that the presidential candidate spouses in 2016 were the two least popular spouses in modern times, the reasons for their diminished level of favorability have more to do with the distinctive ways they challenged the concept of new traditionalism. There are reasons to believe future candidate spouses can and will achieve the strongly favorable review of most of their predecessors.

This book finds that a pivotal force behind the surprising popularity of candidate spouses compared to other national political figures is their ability to generate support from opposite party identifiers. During the 1992 election, Barbara Bush was viewed warmly by most Democrats. Although not as high as the support Barbara Bush received from Democrats, a significant minority of support from opposite party adherents also helps explain the popularity of Michelle Obama and Ann Romney. The original survey data collected for this book indicate that one of the reasons for candidate spouses' broader appeal is that a minority of Americans retain greater sympathy for candidate spouses than other campaign surrogates, recognizing that candidate spouses have not chosen the spotlight but rather have been thrust into it by their partner's political ambitions.

Nevertheless, the American public's continuing drift toward ever higher levels of partisan polarization (Abramowitz and Webster 2016; Campbell 2016; Jacobson 2016) places a clear ceiling on how favorable presidential spouses can be viewed. A comparison of the approval ratings of Barbara Bush and Michelle Obama illustrates this point. While both were quite popular, Michelle Obama could not amass the level of support among Republicans that Barbara Bush was able to amass among Democrats. Indeed, even Ann Romney, who was new to the national political scene in 2012 and almost perfectly embodied the role of traditional candidate spouse, generated some of the most polarized reactions. This is likely a product of the polarized environment more so than anything she did.

The relationship between partisan polarization and new traditionalism involves a set of complex political dynamics. When spouses defy traditional expectations, it does lead to more polarized reactions along partisan lines to some degree. For example, Hillary Clinton in 1992 and Elizabeth Dole in 1996, both came to the position of presidential candidate spouse with significant careers and the news media speculated about their political ambitions. And in return they did produce more polarized reactions than Barbara Bush in 1992 as well as Laura Bush and Tipper Gore in 2000. But challenging traditionalism also tends to lower approval ratings among people in both parties. In 1992, a central reason why Hillary Clinton had approval ratings more than 35 percentage points lower than Barbara Bush was because Democrats as well as Republicans viewed her less favorably than is typical for a Democratic presidential candidate spouse.

The case of Melania Trump is also illustrative. Her low approval ratings are not the result of a particularly polarized response compared to recent presidential candidate spouses. Rather, they are a product of both Republicans and Democrats viewing her less favorably than they viewed her predecessors such as Cindy McCain or Ann Romney. Thus, although the non-traditional aspects of her performance as candidate spouse, as illustrated in the scandals emerging around her, appear to have driven down her approval ratings among both Democrats and Republicans, her decidedly low-profile role may have helped avoid polarization. As discussed in the previous chapter, Melania Trump is the least polarizing candidate spouse along partisan lines since 2000.

Melania Trump's ability to slip through the grasp of polarization to some degree is particularly significant given that the Trump presidency has ushered in a period of even more polarized and vitriolic politics (Sabato 2017). In this sense, the role of first lady and candidate spouse could be more important as ever, as it holds potential to help keep the nation together. As discussed in Chap. 5, Melania Trump was not popular compared to other candidate spouses in recent decades, but since becoming first lady her approving ratings have climbed upward and are now close to 20 points higher than those of her husband. In some ways, the minimal role of Melania Trump, staying far removed from policy and politics—carrying out symbolic responsibilities with impeccable fashion—has allowed her to benefit from some goodwill from Democrats and liberals. Melania Trump has not become a focal point of criticism for Democratic Party elites nor has there been a coordinated effort to undermine her standing in the minds of voters. There seems to be a sense among most Democratic Party leaders that since she "plays by the rules," she should not be fair game for criticism. If she remains detached from major policy discussions or other controversies in the Trump Administration, at the very least her image among Democrats may stabilize and avoid higher levels of polarization than Bill Clinton's extensive political history would have generated had he become first spouse.

Interdependence of Public Opinion Toward Candidate Spouses and the Candidates

Public opinion toward presidential candidate spouses and the candidates themselves remain inextricably intertwined. The data presented in this book delineate two parallel findings pertaining to the concept of independence. On the one hand, the strongest predictors of individual support for spouses are views toward the presidential candidates themselves. Thus, to a large degree, the fate of presidential candidates and their spouses in the eyes of the public is tied together. This is even the case for spouses that are well-known political figures such as Michelle Obama in 2012 and Bill Clinton in 2016. And even though public perceptions of Melania Trump were not as strongly defined by perceptions of her husband as some other spouses, and as may have been expected given her low-profile role in the campaign, attitudes toward Donald Trump remained the most prominent factor shaping evaluations of her. Melania Trump was the least popular spouse in modern polling history, and Donald Trump's unprecedented unpopularity contributed significantly to her lack of support.

Despite their connection to the presidential candidates, the survey results also indicate candidate spouses remain autonomous figures with ratings that typically but not always rise above the candidates' own favorability. In 1992, First Lady Barbara Bush maintained an incredible reservoir of goodwill with American public in the face of very poor approval ratings for President George H.W. Bush. And while Barack Obama was viewed slightly more favorably than Michelle Obama during the 2008 election and the brief honeymoon phase of his presidency, for the remainder of their time in the White House, Michelle Obama consistently retained favorable ratings higher than her husband's ratings. The two other exceptions to this trend are telling. Hillary Clinton in 1996 and Teresa Heinz Kerry in 2004 both chose to present themselves more autonomously and less traditionally than other candidate spouses, and they both ended with favorable averages lower than those of their husbands. By embracing new traditionalism, candidate spouses have the ability to remain more popular figures than their spouses in a highly combative political climate.

The concept of independence is also on display when looking at the different trajectories of public opinion toward Melania Trump and Donald Trump during their time in public life together. During the 2016 election, Melania Trump's unfavorable ratings, while at historic lows for candidate spouses, never reached the dismal level that President Trump's consistently did. After the election and across her first year as first lady, Melania Trump has seen an uptick in public support, while President Trump has generally trended downward since he was inaugurated. Thus, Melania Trump is proving successful at carving out her own image to some degree.

Given the assortment of controversies that have plagued the Trump Administration, it remains an open question as to whether Melania Trump's standing in the eyes of the public can continue to trend in a positive direction or whether she will suffer a backlash. Thus far, she has avoided any major missteps in her own right that might do long-lasting damage to her own personal standing. By maintaining favorable ratings higher than the ratings of her husband, Melania Trump holds the potential to be an asset to her husband in his presidency (Wright 2016b). Whether she chooses to use her relative popularity to advance her husband's agenda or improve his image, however, is yet to be seen.

Future Opportunities for Research on Candidate Spouses

This study represents the most comprehensive examination of public attitudes toward presidential candidate spouses in the modern era. Despite the considerable amount of data presented in the previous chapters, this book is far from the last word on this topic. A number of different ways exist for this subject to be explored in the future. Scholars of public opinion, gender politics, presidential campaigns, and the presidency itself have many opportunities to delve more deeply into to the contours of public opinion toward presidential spouses.

One area future research can investigate more thoroughly is public opinion toward presidential candidate spouses during the party primary campaign season. This study focuses primarily on public evaluations of the spouses of the two major party nominees in the general election. This decision makes sense since they are the most publicly visible spouses, and the public opinion data in existence only ask consistently about the spouses of the major party nominees. However, since spouses play a role in presidential campaigns prior to the kickoff of the general election, there is much to be gleaned from gauging reactions to the spouses during the primary process.

One of the major advantages is that public reactions to the spouses can be assessed in the absence of partisanship as a cue. Although many spouses can rise above partisan polarization more easily than the candidates themselves, the evidence in this book demonstrates that party identification is a major driver of how individuals view the spouses. In the context of a nomination contest, primary or caucus voters cannot rely on partisanship as a shortcut in formulating perceptions toward political figures at this stage of the process (Abramson et al. 1992). The exclusion of the partisan heuristic allows researchers to more easily determine what other variables are central in shaping how individuals feel about the spouses.

Another benefit of studying public opinion in the presidential nomination process is that it allows for the study of a more diverse cross-section of presidential candidate spouses. The 2016 election provides an excellent example of this diversity. As discussed in Chap. 5, Melania Trump and Bill Clinton were unique spouses in a variety of different ways. Yet, as distinctive as they were, they could not encompass the entire diversity represented by the spouses of the leading contenders for president in the Democratic and Republican parties. This diverse set of career backgrounds spanned the gamut from former university president Jane Sanders on the Democratic side, to Goldman Sachs, investment manager at Heidi Cruz and full-time homemaker Jeanette Rubio on the Republican side. Besides a variety of career backgrounds, they represented racial and ethnic diversity, as Jeanette Rubio, Columba Bush, and Candy Carson were all women of color. The 2016 spouses also included another male, former AT&T executive Frank Fiorina, husband of Carly Fiorina.[1]

The major hurdle to further exploration of candidate spouses at the primary stage is the limited amount of public opinion data available to conduct systematic analysis. Media organizations rarely ask any questions about the spouses of presidential candidates until the nominees of the two major parties have been selected. Unless and until they begin to query the public about their reactions to presidential candidate spouses during the primary process, the dearth of available data will stymie the efforts to do research in this area. Academics can fill some of the void by securing research funds to ask questions on nationally representative surveys, as was undertaken in this book project, but there are simply not enough resources to build a large enough data base without a significant contribution from the media. With newspapers and television news on the decline and a plethora of other issues that need to be polled on during the presidential primary campaign, it will not be easy to get this effort off the ground. Nevertheless, given their strategic importance in campaigns, a more complete picture of how presidential candidate spouses are viewed through the process paints a more robust portrait of the public opinion dynamics associated with this topic.

Another line of potential research in this area is to consider public perceptions of the spouses of vice-presidential candidates. Although they are far less visible political actors than presidential spouses, they have attracted more scrutiny in recent years and play a role in the campaign apparatus during the election process. While some are more visible than others, they also provide a diverse set of political actors that can further shed on light on many of the theoretical frames outlined in this book. Individuals like Todd Palin (husband of 2008 Republican vice-presidential nominee Sarah Palin), Jill Biden, and 2016 vice-presidential candidate spouses Anne Holton and Karen Pence provide a broad template of personalities and backgrounds from which to gain a better appreciation of the public views of the spouses of major political figures in this country. Jill Biden in particular would be interesting to study as she continued her work as a community college professor, while her husband, Joe Biden, served for vice-president for two terms. The lack of attention to this issue suggests that the public is less concerned about the degree to which vice-presidential spouses conform to traditional expectations, but public opinion data would be useful in developing these ideas further.

Finally, examining public perceptions of political spouses from a comparative perspective could provide a contribution to the scholarship on this topic. This comparative context could be international by looking at how citizens from nations outside the United States view the spouses of candidates for the position of chief executive in their country. It could also consist of studies examining the spouses of candidates for governor or US senate at the state level in the United States. Each of these comparative contexts can supply additional insight to the evidence compiled in this book.

Exploring these additional avenues should supplement, not supplant, continued focus on public opinion toward the spouses of the presidential candidates nominated by the two major parties. The 2020 election could provide another male spouse, as several of the early names mentioned prominently for the Democratic presidential nomination are women including Senators Elizabeth Warren, Kamala Harris, Amy Klobuchar, and Kirsten Gillibrand. With spouses that have a much lower profile than Bill Clinton, if one of them was nominated, it would allow for a much different political context to gauge public reactions to a male spouse of a major party nominee for president. If President Donald Trump is nominated once again by the Republican Party, scholars can determine to what extent Melania Trump has benefited from the incumbency advantage of serving as first lady for a full term. These developments in 2020 and beyond warrant continued monitoring of public opinion toward the spouses of presidential candidates because they will continue to occupy a prominent role in the political operations of those who seek to serve in the White House. A failure to account for how the American public views them will result in an incomplete understanding of modern presidential campaign dynamics.

Note

1. A former Hewlett Packard CEO, Carly Fiorina not only sought the Republican presidential nomination in 2016 but after dropping "race" out, she also briefly served as the vice-presidential running mate of the US Senator Ted Cruz (Lawless 2016).

Bibliography

Abramowitz, Alan I., and Stephen Webster. 2016. The Rise of Negative Partisanship and the Nationalization of U.S. Elections in the 21st Century. *Electoral Studies* 41 (1): 12–22.

Abramson, Paul R., John H. Aldrich, Paul Paolino, and David W. Rohde. 1992. Sophisticated Voting in the 1988 Presidential Primaries. *American Political Science Review* 86 (1): 55–69.

Ansolabehere, Stephen, and James M. Snyder Jr. 2004. The Incumbency Advantage in U.S. Elections: An Analysis of State and Federal Offices, 1942–2000. *Election Law Journal: Rules, Politics, and Policy* 1 (15): 315–338.

Bobo, Lawrence, and Franklin D. Gilliam Jr. 1990. Race, Sociopolitical Participation, and Black Empowerment. *American Political Science Review* 84 (2): 377–393.

Borrelli, MaryAnne. 2011. *The Politics of the President's Wife*. College Station, TX: Texas A&M University Press.

Burrell, Barbara. 2001. *Public Opinion, The First Ladyship, and Hillary Rodham Clinton*. New York: Routledge.

Burrell, Barbara, Laurel Elder, and Brian Frederick. 2011. From Hillary to Michelle: Public Opinion and the Spouses of Presidential Candidates. *Presidential Studies Quarterly* 41 (1): 156–176.

Campbell, James E. 2016. *Polarized: Making Sense of a Divided America*. Princeton, NJ: Princeton University Press.

Cilliza, Chris. 2017. Melania is the Most Popular Trump. *CNN.com*, September 21. Accessed November, 2017.

Dittmar, Kelly. 2015. Gender Expectations and the Presidential Partnership. Center for American Women and Politics, Presidential Gender Watch. Accessed November 7, 2017. http://presidentialgenderwatch.org/gender-expectations-and-the-presidential-partnership/

Dolan, Kathleen. 2008. Is There a "Gender Affinity Effect" in American Politics? Information, Affect and Candidate Sex in U.S. House Elections. *Political Research Quarterly* 61 (1): 79–89.

Duerst-Lahti, Georgia. 2014. Presidential Elections: Gendered Space and the Case of 2012. In *Gender and Elections: Shaping the Future of American Politics*, ed. Susan J. Carroll and Richard L. Fox, 3rd ed., 16–48. Cambridge: Cambridge University Press.

Elder, Laurel, and Brian Frederick. 2017. Perceptions of Candidate Spouses in the 2012 Presidential Election: The Role of Gender, Race, Religion, and Partisanship. *Politics, Groups, and Identities*: 1–22. https://doi.org/10.1080/21565503.2017.1338969

Fandos, Nicholas. 2017. First Family's Needs Strain Secret Service. *New York Times*, April 6.

Gfk Omni Survey. 2017. KnowledgePanel (KP) OmniWeb Survey conducted by GFK Custom Research LLC, September 15–17.

Goodin, Emily. 2017. Melania Trump Inching Toward Spotlight. *RealClearPolitics.com*, August 15. Accessed November, 2017.

Jacobson, Gary C. 2016. Polarization, Gridlock, and Presidential Campaign Politics in 2016. *The Annals of the American Academy of Political and Social Science* 667 (1): 226–246.

Jacobson, Gary C., and Jamie L. Carson. 2015. *The Politics of Congressional Elections*. 9th ed. Lanham, MD: Rowman and Littlefield.

Knuckey, Jonathan, and Myunghee Kim. 2016. Evaluations of Michelle Obama as First Lady: The Role Racial Resentment. *Presidential Studies Quarterly* 46 (2): 365–386.

Lawless, Jennifer. 2016. Fiorina Just a Pawn in Cynical Game Cruz Won't Win. April 27. Accessed November 5, 2017. http://www.cnn.com/2016/04/27/opinions/fiorina-cruz-lawless/index.html.

Mandziuk, Roseann M. 2017. Whither the Good Wife? 2016 Presidential Candidate Spouses in the Gendered Spaces of Contemporary Politics. *Quarterly Journal of Speech* 103 (1–2): 136–159.

Mansbridge, Jane. 1999. Should Blacks Represent Blacks and Women Represent Women? A Contingent 'Yes'. *The Journal of Politics* 61 (3): 628–657.

Mayhew, David R. 2008. Incumbency Advantage in U.S. Presidential Elections: The Historical Record. *Presidential Studies Quarterly* 123 (2): 201–228.

Puente, Maria. 2017. All the Stuff Melania Trump has done in Her First 100 Days. *USA Today*, May 9, 2017.

Sabato, Larry J. 2017. The Election that Broke All or At Least Most of the Rules. In *Trumped the Election that Broke All of the Rules*, ed. Larry J. Sabato, Kyle Kondik, and Geoffrey Skelly, 1–29. Lanham, MD: Rowman and Littlefield.

Simien, Evelyn. 2016. *Historic Firsts: How Symbolic Empowerment Changes U.S. Politics*. New York: Oxford University Press.

Thompson, Krissah. 2017. Melania Trump Condemns Bullying—And Raises Some Eyebrows—In Her First U.N. Speech. *Washington Post*, September 20. Accessed November 7, 2017.

Thrush, Glenn, and Maggie Haberman. 2017. Trump and Staff Rethink Tactics After Stumbles. *The New York Times*.

Troy, Gil. 2006. *Hillary Clinton: Polarizing First Lady*. Lawrence, KS: Kansas University Press.

Vigil, Tammy R. 2014. Feminine Views in the Feminine Style: Convention Speeches by Presidential Nominees' Spouses. *Southern Communication Journal* 79: 327–346.

Weiner, Jennifer. 2017. Want Melania Trump in the White House? Pay Her. *The New York Times, op-ed*, February 18, 2017.

Wright, Lauren. 2016a. *On Behalf of the President: Presidential Spouses and White House Communications Strategy Today*. Santa Barbara, CA: Praeger.

———. 2016b. Here's Evidence that Melania Trump could Actually Boost Donald Trump's Popularity. *Washington Post*, March 30, 2016.

Wright, Lauren. 2017. Melania Trump Refuses to Act Like a First Lady. Good for Her. *Washington Post*, January 19.

Index[1]

[1] Note: Page number followed by 'n' refer to notes.

L. Elder et al., *American Presidential Candidate Spouses*,
https://doi.org/10.1007/978-3-319-73879-6

S

T

V

W